brilliant knits

brilliant knits

25 contemporary designs

BRANDON MABLY

from the Kaffe Fassett studio

The Taunton Press

I would like to dedicate this book to all yarn shops worldwide for their countless hours of encouragement and devotion to this humble but life-enhancing craft.

First published in 2001

1 3 5 7 9 10 8 6 4 2

Photographer: Joey Toller
Stylist: Brandon Mably
Pattern writer: Sharon Brant
Pattern checker: Marilyn Wilson
Designer: Christine Wood
Illustrator: Antony Duke

The Taunton Press
Inspiration for hands-on living™

First published in the United Kingdom in 2001 by Ebury Press, Random House, 20 Vauxhall Bridge Road, London SW1V 2SA

The Taunton Press, Inc.
63 South Main St.
PO Box 5506
Newtown, CT 06470-5506
www.taunton.com

Distributed by Publishers Group West

ISBN 1-56158-511-4

Color separation by Colorlito, Milan
Printed and bound in Singapore

CONTENTS

Foreword by Kaffe Fassett

What are the ingredients that combine to make a good knitwear designer? A facility for technique certainly makes a difference when it comes to designing patterns for others to follow and, of course, a good feeling for colour also comes very high in my book. But first and foremost, a good knitwear designer must have an eye for style, which can only be obtained by years of intense looking and experimenting. Brandon popped out of the womb with one of the sharpest eyes for style I've ever come across. He takes a prodigious amount of joy in people-watching and there is little that escapes his laser beam.

Having no education in design, what is most noticeable about Brandon is his swift willingness to learn from everything put before him. He came to my studio back in 1991 with the vague and ambitious notion of making some order in the place. 'You'll have to invent the job,' I told him as I rushed about trying to design, answer telephones, cook for workers, stitch large tapestry commissions and knit swatches for the next Rowan season. Brandon calmly – but with energy and speed – took over the telephones, cooked the meals and arranged the masses of lectures, workshops and exhibitions I was involved with. Seeing how much joy he took in new experiences like museums, theatres and the odd trip away, I began to take on more work in foreign destinations. I trained him to knit, do needlepoint, hook rag rugs and grout mosaics. Soon we were travelling the world doing workshops, where he proved an inspiring teacher. Exotic countries like South Africa, Japan, Guatemala and India filled our designers' eyes with an explosion of colour and pattern. After a few years of this he took over the knitting workshops altogether, learning so much (as we teachers do) from students struggling to grasp colour and technique.

One day Brandon put all this knowledge and influence into one of his first knitwear designs, which I liked so much I included it in my own book *Kaffe's Classics*. Needlepoint and rag rug designs followed, but his stylish eye brought him back again and again to knitwear design. *Vogue Knitting Magazine* was quick to grab his use of colour and he is now a regular design contributor.

I feel sure you will enjoy the variety of moods and levels of design found among these pages. Some are for beginners, others are more challenging – but most are done in basic stocking stitch. This first book of Brandon's is a fine launch indeed for a most natural talent.

Kaffe Fassett

Introduction

Who is Brandon Mably you may wonder? The answer is that I'm a guy brought up in a small seaside town on the coast of South Wales who is crazy about colour and design and enthusiastic to share my pleasures with others. Fine appearance has been bred into me from an early age starting with my Irish grandparents, who were always immaculately dressed, and my mother, who made fine clothes when my sister and I were children, some of which she still has. I have also always been attracted to personalities with an individual flair for clothing. One of my fondest childhood memories is seeing a neighbour doing her grocery shopping in a blue striped kaftan that her husband had bought her from the Far East – how proud she looked to be wearing it.

But why knitting you may also wonder? As a child, my first impressions of wool were unusually fostered by visits to our local sweet shop, which also served as the yarn shop. Next to all the glass jars containing delicious lurid coloured candies were floor-to-ceiling dark wooden shelves, wire racks and old glass cabinets quite simply bulging with vividly coloured balls, spools and hanks of knitting yarn. A great way to get children into a yarn shop at an early age, wouldn't you say? I also have distant memories of knitting lessons being taught to the boys as well as girls as part of our school curriculum. But sadly my only lasting recollection of the lessons are of the deep smoky pink coloured plastic knitting needles that I used. It was only in my early twenties that I discovered knitting was a delightfully simple and unexpected way of playing with colour.

I started my career in knitwear design back in the early nineties when I turned from professional cooking to designing. This unusual career change came about through an accidental meeting with the man who really put knitting on the map – Kaffe Fassett. The moment I first walked into his studio I was struck by the walls, which were braced with shelves from floor to ceiling housing spools of yarn divided into their colour groups. The floorboards were strewn with Turkish and Islamic carpets and there were piles of needlepoint cushions smothered in images of vegetables, animals and flowers. Waist-high Chinese urns and collections of decorative ceramics filled every corner and there was a veritable bank of huge, wide open wicker baskets stuffed with yet more balls of wool, cotton, silk and chenille yarns; all in smouldering tones of colour and various textures. Cupboards and drawers burst with neatly stacked, highly patterned knitted garments. It was like entering that sweet shop for the first time all over again.

This was my first brush with the labyrinth of a creative mind and something I knew I wanted to be a part of. My apprenticeship took place as I attended to the organizing and running of the studio, while watching Kaffe and his team design and execute commissions and create the books for which he is now famous. Kaffe would often ask for my input on the designs he was creating and, liking my intuitive answers, he encouraged me to try designing myself. As Kaffe's schedule filled up with other tasks, I slowly took over teaching his knitting workshops. These teaching posts took me to the varied and exotic worlds of Iceland, Africa, Japan, North and South America, where everything about the cultures stimulated my designer's eye. I entered Kaffe Fassett's world with no experience but soon discovered I had a natural instinct for colour and design. This has grown

as I have had the opportunity of teaching and helping others. And there is nothing more rewarding than encouraging other people to have a go themselves. It has taught me one thing beyond all others – most people have buried in them a sense of colour and design.

I'm fairly new to the knitting world and quite basic in my approach to technique. In the process of learning to knit I realized that the cables, fancy stitches and unusual shapes would distract from the impact I wanted to create. So I concentrated on using good old stocking stitch and the fabulous intarsia and Fair Isle techniques (described in detail on pages 10–11) that enable you to control colour changes and knit in your ends as you work. Keeping the shape of the garments simple and classic allows for any sizing to be easily incorporated. And now, here I am throwing out some ideas for you to knit up but, like any good recipe, feel free to change the ingredients to suit your own palette and shape. All the garments are knitted in the wonderful colour ranges of Rowan and Jaegar yarns, mostly using basic stocking stitch. Take advantage of all the yarns you have available and if they are not on your doorstep look a little further, remembering that there is always the Internet and mail order. When styling a garment, it is also important to keep in mind that a colour scheme can be enriched or diminished by the colours accompanying it through buttons and other accessories.

I hope you enjoy this book as much as I have enjoyed putting it together.

Brandon Mably

BASIC INFORMATION

CHOOSING YARNS

If you want to work any of the patterns in your own colourway, ignoring the colours I've specified then, of course, you can do so. However, if you're nervous about choosing colours, or if you want something exactly like the garment pictured, then use the yarns specified. I've recommended a yarn type and colour for all patterns and listed the amount needed of each. That amount is never less than 25g (1oz) since it's impossible to buy in smaller quantities, so there will be lots left over and these can be added to your stockpile of yarn. Try to buy the yarn specified in the pattern;

however, if you prefer to use a substitute, buy a yarn that is the same weight and has the same tension or stitch gauge (see below). It is essential to check metreage or yardage. Yarn that weighs the same may have different lengths, and you may need to buy more or less yarn. Check the ball band (yarn wrapper) on the yarn. Most labels now carry all the information you need about fibre content, washing instructions, weight and metreage or yardage. Some of them will tell you the needle sizes to use and the standard tension (or stitch size) these create.

TENSION (GAUGE)

I sympathise with knitters who are impatient to get on with the job and do not want to spend time on tension samples. However, the same instructions in the hands of tight or loose knitters can end up in a child's jacket or a huge coat. So the dreaded tension squares are absolutely essential if hours of work are not to be wasted.

'Tension' is the number of stitches and rows to a centimetre (inch) that should be obtained on the given needles, yarn and stitch pattern and is also known as 'stitch gauge' or 'gauge'. The tension determines the measurements of a garment so it is very important that you obtain the same number of rows and stitches as given in each pattern. A small difference over 10 centimetres (4 inches) can add up to a considerable amount over the complete width of the knitted garment.

To check your tension, work a sample at least 10 centimetres (4 inches) square using the given yarn, needles and stitch pattern used for the garment. Press the tension swatch lightly on a flat surface, but do not stretch the sample. Using a ruler, measure and mark the number of stitches and rows in the central area of the sample and check this number against the set tension. If you have too many stitches try another swatch using larger needles, but if you have too few stitches try again with smaller needles. Remember also that where the instructions give the tension 'over pattern', then the tension square must be worked from the chart and the colours handled as specified. Also, try to use several of the yarns specified (if any combinations are called for, make sure to work them in the tension sample).

HANDLING MANY COLOURS

Many of the patterns in this book look infinitely complicated, rich and intricate, which may lead some of you to think they are extremely difficult to knit. In fact they are well within the capabilities of the average knitter. I only ever use stocking stitch and ribs, with the occasional edging of crochet, moss stitch or garter stitch, so all you really have to think about are the colours.

Handling a large number of colours is something that worries a lot of knitters. In fact, it's not as difficult as it seems. Many of the patterns only use two or three colours to a row – it's just that those colours change frequently and that's what makes them seem complicated. The most important thing when knitting with lots of colours is to handle the yarns properly. There are two main methods: intarsia and Fair Isle.

INTARSIA

The intarsia method is mostly used where there are lots of different colours in a row, many of them used in only one or two places. Instead of being carried across the back of the work, these yarns are simply worked in their place then left hanging until the next row, and the next colour is knitted. In most cases, it is important to twist the two yarns together at the colour change to avoid holes (this is especially important when working vertical lines).

The easiest way to work intarsia is to wind off small lengths of yarn for each coloured area to be worked. When knitting, link one yarn to the next by twisting the two yarns around each other once at the change over point on the wrong side of the work. This will avoid gaps. All ends should then be darned in along the colour lines. Never weave into a row as this will show through to the right side. Be particularly careful to keep an even tension.

CHANGING COLOURS ON A VERTICAL LINE

CHANGING COLOURS ON A RIGHT DIAGONAL

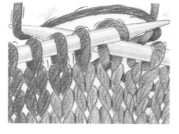

CHANGING COLOURS ON A LEFT DIAGONAL

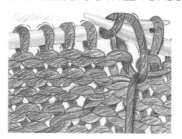

FAIR ISLE

Knitting-in is really my term for what Fair Isle knitters call 'weaving-in'. When two or more colours are used repeatedly in a row, the yarn not being worked is carried across the back until it is next needed. If only a few stitches are spanned, then it can simply be looped, or 'stranded', across (very loosely). If there are more than about five stitches to span, it should be woven under and over the working yarn as you go, so that the looped yarns are caught at the back of the work (I always operate these

'floating' yarns with my left hand). Some knitters knit-in in this way on every other stitch, but I find it sufficient to do it on every third stitch or so.

It is very important that the 'stranding' or 'weaving-in' is done at a relaxed even tension or the knitting will pucker. In any case, this method does pull in a great deal more than the intarsia method, and therefore results in quite a different tension, so it's vital not to get the two confused.

STRANDING ON A KNIT ROW

STRANDING ON A PURL ROW

KNITTING-IN ON A KNIT ROW

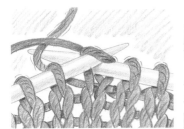 

KNITTING-IN ON A PURL ROW

1 To knit-in yarn on a knit stitch, insert the right-hand needle into the next stitch and lay the yarn to be knitted-in over the right-hand needle. Knit the stitch with working yarn, taking it under the yarn not in use and making sure you do not catch this strand into the knitted stitch.
2 Knit the next stitch with the working yarn, taking it over the yarn being knitted-in. Continue like this, weaving the loose colour over and under the working yarn alternately with each stitch until you need to use it again.

1 To knit-in yarn on a purl stitch, insert the right-hand needle into the next stitch and lay the yarn to be knitted-in over the right-hand needle. Purl the stitch with working yarn, taking it under not in use and making sure you do not catch this strand into the purled stitch.
2 Purl the next stitch with the working yarn, taking it over the yarn being knitted-in. Continue like this, weaving the loose colour over and under the working yarn alternately with each stitch until you need to use it again.

KNITTING-IN ENDS

I also knit in all the ends of yarn as I work. This saves hours of laborious darning in after the knitting is over. It's basically the same as knitting in the floating yarns. What you do is this; when joining in a new colour leave ends of about 8cm (3 in) on the old yarn and the new; work the next two stitches with the new yarn then, holding both ends in your left hand, lay them over the working yarn and work the next

stitch; now insert the right-hand needle into the next stitch in the usual way, then bring the ends (still holding them in your left hand) up over the point of the right-hand needle and work this stitch past the ends. Carry on in this way laying the ends over the working yarns on every second or third stitch and knitting past the ends on the following stitch until they are completely knitted in.

WORKING WITH MANAGEABLE LENGTHS

This is the hottest tip for speed and the preservation of your sanity when knitting with many colours. The different yarns inevitably get tangled at the back of the work, so I rarely have balls or bobbins attached. Instead I break off short lengths of 60–100cm (2–3 ft), depending on the area to

be covered, and use these. As they get tangled it's easy just to pull through the colour you want. When more of a colour is required tie on another length, knitting in all the ends as you work. This method also encourages you to introduce subtle changes of tone.

SWISS DARNING (DUPLICATE STITCH)

Swiss darning, or duplicate stitch, is a great boon when knitting with colours. You simply cover a stitch or several stitches with yarn in a different colour after the knitting has been completed. This means that

you can correct mistakes without having to unravel your work, you can add extra colours to give a scheme just a little more lift, and you can mask a colour that isn't working.

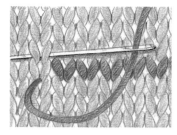

1 Thread a blunt-ended needle with yarn the same weight as the stitch you are darning over. Bring the needle out at the base of the first stitch you want to cover, then take it under the base of the stitch above.

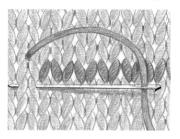

2 Take the needle back through the base of the first stitch and out at the base of the next stitch. Continue to cover each stitch this way.

READING PATTERNS

Most of the patterns in this book are one size. However, where there are several sizes, the smallest size is given first in the instructions and appears outside of the round ( ) brackets (or parantheses); the larger

sizes are given inside the brackets. Work pattern instructions given in square [ ] brackets the number of times stated afterwards. Where 0 appears, no stitches or rows are worked for this size.

CHARTS

Most of the patterns are worked from charts. Each square on a chart represents a stitch, and each horizontal row of squares represents a row of knitting. The first row of the chart usually represents the first row of the knitting. You read knit rows from right to left and purl rows from left to right (unless otherwise stated); and you start at the bottom of the chart and work up (unless otherwise stated).

The symbols on the chart refer to the colours or yarns to be used for those stitches. In some cases there will also be a colour sequence table or key to the symbols which will tell you exactly what colour to use for each stitch. Sometimes the chart for the whole garment is given; alternatively, only a section will be given and it may be necessary to

repeat it several times. If the colour pattern is a repeated design, the chart will indicate how many stitches are in each repeat. The stitches before and after the repeat are the edge stitches. You knit the edge stitches at the beginning of the row, then knit the repeat as many times as necessary until you reach the edge stitches at the end of the row. All this will be explained on the charts themselves or in the instructions.

Once you get used to them, charts are much easier to work from than written instructions because you can see exactly what you are supposed to be doing. Often the first few rows are written out just to get you started. To help keep your place, cover the part of the chart not yet worked with a piece of stiff card.

ABBREVIATIONS

The following abbreviations are used throughout the patterns:

alt	alternate(ly)
approx	approximately
beg	begin(ning)
cm	centimetre(s)
cont	continu(e)(ing)
dec	decreas(e)(ing)
foll	follow(s)(ing)
g	gram(me)(s)
in	inch(es)
inc	increas(e)(ing)
inc 1 st	increase one st by working into the front and back of the stitch
K	knit
K up	pick up and knit
M1	make one by picking up the loop lying between the stitch just worked and next stitch and working into the back of it
mm	millimetre(s)
oz	ounce(s)
P	purl

patt	pattern
psso	pass slipped stitch over
rem	remain(s)(ing)
rep	repeat(s)(ing)
RS	right side of work
skpo	slip one, knit one, pass slipped stitch over
sl	slip
st(s)	stitch(es)
st st	stocking stitch (stockinette stitch)
tbl	through back of loop(s)
tog	together
wrap st	slip next st onto right-hand needle, bring yarn forward between needles, slip st back onto left-hand needle, turn. (When working back across the wrapped sts take loop made and stitch together as one.)
WS	wrong side of work
yb	yarn back
yf	yarn forward
yon	yarn over needle
yrn	yarn round needle (yarn over)

FINISHING

Some things can make or break a garment as far as I'm concerned. Many of these are to do with the way it is finished. Working edgings too loosely or too tightly has, above all else, given hand knitting a bad name. After working an edging for the first time, we often find that we need more or fewer stitches and have to unpick and reknit it, so don't be afraid to redo them if they don't work out initially. These patterns tell you exactly how many stitches to pick up (for neckbands, collars, and so on), but the essential thing is to space the stitches evenly along the appropriate edge.

Plain wide button and buttonhole bands are another of my bête noires. I like them to be patterned or striped or, if they have to be plain, as narrow as possible. This is why we almost always make our buttonholes on the same row as we pick up the stitches. Some of you

may find this a bit tricky, in which case do make your buttonholes in the usual way, but add stripes or patterns to avoid that wide blank strip down the front of the garment. I like the buttons to all but disappear into a garment while still having a quiet life of their own, and I'm always combing markets to find special ones.

Good pressing also makes an enormous difference, especially to patterned knitting. Since I use mixtures of yarns I always play safe and press with a steam iron or over a damp cloth. I don't like to flatten the knitting completely so I try not to be too heavy-handed. We also pay special attention to pressing seams and hems. I use either backstitch or mattress stitch when sewing up garments to produce an almost invisible seam. All seams should be sewn with a large blunt-ended yarn or tapestry needle to avoid splitting the yarn.

BACKSTITCH

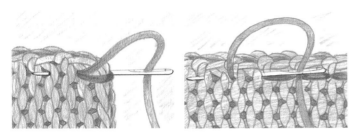

1 With right sides placed side by side, secure the seam by taking the needle twice around the outer edges from back to front. Then bring the needle through both thicknesses no more than 1cm (¹/₄ in) from where the yarn last came out.
2 Insert the needle back into the point where the yarn came out from the last stitch and bring the needle back through the same distance ahead of the emerging yarn. Repeat these steps, keeping stitches of uniform length and in an absolutely straight line.

MATTRESS STITCH

With the right sides of the knitting facing you, insert the needle under the horizontal bar between the first stitch and next stitch. Then insert the needle under the same bar on the other piece. Continue to do this, drawing up the thread to form the seam.

CIRCULAR NEEDLES

I almost always use circular needles or twinpins. Sometimes you have to use them (or double-pointed knitting needles) for working neckbands in the round, but they are also much more convenient than the conventional pairs of straight knitting needles even for flat knitting. When making garments in one piece (all the jackets and

coats in this book are made this way), the knitting can get very heavy. With straight knitting needles this weight is taken by your arms; with circular needles it rests much more comfortably in your lap. Circular needles can also hold far more stitches than ordinary straight knitting needles.

CARING FOR YOUR GARMENT

Taking care of your knitted garments is important. If you have invested time and effort into knitting them, you want them to look good for as long as possible. Follow these simple care guidelines for the best results.

Washing and drying your knitting

Check the ball band on your yarn for washing instructions. Many yarns can now be machine washed on a delicate wool cycle. You may find it helpful to make a note of the measurements of the garment, such as the width and length, prior to washing. After washing, lay the garment flat and check the measurements again to see if they are the same. If not, smooth and pat it back into shape.

If hand washing, use soap flakes specially created for hand knits and warm, rather than hot, water. Handle the knits gently in the water – do not rub or wring because this can felt the fabric. Rinse well to get rid of any soap, and squeeze out excess water. You may need to get rid of more water by rolling the garment in a towel, or you can use the delicate spin cycle of the washing machine.

Dry the garment by laying it out flat on top of a towel to absorb moisture, smooth and pat into shape. Do not dry knits near direct heat such as radiator.

Store your knits loosely folded to allow the air to circulate.

Basic information

Hints for American knitters

American knitters may have a few problems in working from English patterns and vice versa. The following tables and glossaries should prove useful.

UK	US
Aran wool	'fisherman' yarn
ball band	yarn wrapper or label
brackets, round	parentheses
cast off	bind off
catch down	tack down
DK (double knitting)	a yarn weight between sport and worsted
double crochet	single crochet
double moss stitch	double seed stitch
every alternate row	every other row
moss stitch	seed stitch
stocking stitch	stockinette stitch
Swiss darning	duplicate stitch
tension	gauge
welt	lower borders on sweater front and back
yarn forward (yf)	yarn over (yo), or yarn to front of work between two needles
yarn round needle (yrn)	yarn over (yo)

All other terms are the same in both countries.

UK/US yarn equivalents

Only three types of yarn are used in this book. The following table shows their approximate equivalents in terms of thickness. However, it is always essential to check your tension.

UK	US
4 ply	fingering
double knitting	between sport and worsted
Aran/medium weight	fisherman/medium weight

Metric conversion tables

Length (to the nearest 1/4 in)				Weight (rounded up to the nearest 1/4 oz)	
cm	in	cm	in	g	oz
1	1/2	55	213/4	25	1
2	3/4	60	231/2	50	2
3	11/4	65	251/2	100	33/4
4	11/2	70	271/2	150	51/2
5	2	75	291/2	200	71/4
6	21/2	80	311/2	250	9
7	23/4	85	331/2	300	103/4
8	3	90	351/2	350	121/2
9	31/2	95	371/2	400	141/4
10	4	100	391/2	450	16
11	41/4	110	431/2	500	173/4
12	43/4	120	47	550	191/2
13	5	130	511/4	600	211/4
14	51/2	140	55	650	23
15	6	150	59	700	243/4
16	61/4	160	63	750	261/2
17	63/4	170	67	800	281/4
18	7	180	703/4	850	30
19	71/2	190	743/4	900	313/4
20	8	200	783/4	950	333/4
25	93/4	210	823/4	1000	351/2
30	113/4	220	861/2	1200	421/4
35	133/4	230	901/2	1400	491/4
40	153/4	240	941/2	1600	561/2
45	173/4	250	981/2	1800	631/2
50	193/4	300	118	2000	701/2

Needle size conversion table

The needle sizes given in the patterns are recommended starting points for making tension samples. The needle size actually used should be that on which the stated tension (gauge) is obtained.

Metric	US	Old UK and Canadian
2mm	0	14
21/4mm	1	13
23/4mm	2	12
3mm	2–3	11
31/4mm	3	10
33/4mm	5	9
4mm	6	8
41/2mm	7	7
5mm	8	6
51/2mm	9	5
6mm	10	4
61/2mm	101/2	3
7mm	101/2	2
71/2mm	11	1
8mm	11	0
9mm	13	00
10mm	15	000

YARN INFORMATION

Rowan and Jaegar Yarns

The following Rowan and Jaeger yarns have been used for the knitting patterns in this book. See addresses below for obtaining these yarns. If you are purchasing a substitute yarn for the patterns, be sure to calculate the number of balls or hanks required by the number of metres or yards per ball rather than by the yarn weight.

Rowan 4 ply Cotton
very lightweight cotton yarn (US fingering); 100% cotton; approximately 170m (185 yd) per 50g/1³/₄oz ball

Rowan Cotton Glacé
lightweight cotton yarn (US sport); 100% cotton; approximately 115m (125 yd) per 50g/1³/₄oz ball

Rowan DK Soft
medium-weight wool yarn (between US sport and worsted); 85% wool and 15% polyamide; approximately 175m (191 yd) per 50g/1³/₄oz ball

Rowan DK Tweed
medium-weight wool yarn (between US sport and worsted); 50% merino wool, 25% alpaca wool and 25% viscose/rayon; approximately 175m (191 yd) per 50g/1³/₄oz ball

Rowan Felted Tweed
medium-weight wool yarn (between US sport and worsted); 50% merino wool, 25% alpaca wool and 25% viscose/rayon; approximately 175m (191 yd) per 50g/1³/₄oz ball

Rowan Fine Cotton Chenille
lightweight cotton yarn (US sport); 89% cotton; 11% polyester; approximately 160m (175 yd) per 50g/1³/₄oz ball

Rowan Handknit DK Cotton
medium-weight cotton yarn (between US sport and worsted); 100% cotton; approximately 85m (93 yd) per 50g/1³/₄oz ball

Rowan True 4 ply Botany
very lightweight wool yarn (US fingering); 100% pure new wool; approximately 170m (186 yd) per 50g/1³/₄oz ball

Rowan Wool Cotton
medium-weight wool and cotton yarn (between US sport and worsted); 50% merino wool and 50% cotton; approximately 113m (123 yd) per 50g/1³/₄oz ball

Jaeger Alpaca
very lightweight weight wool yarn (US fingering); 100% alpaca wool; approximately 184m (201 yd) per 50g/1³/₄oz ball

Jaeger Cashmere
very lightweight wool yarn (US fingering); 90% cashmere and 10% polyamide; approximately 98m (107 yd) per 25g/1oz ball

Jaeger Matchmaker Merino 4 ply
very lightweight wool yarn (US fingering); 100% merino wool; approximately 183m (200 yd) per 50g/1³/₄oz ball

Jaeger Matchmaker Merino DK
medium-weight wool yarn (between US sport and worsted); 100% merino wool; approximately 120m (131 yd) per 50g/1³/₄oz ball

Jaeger Pure Cotton
lightweight cotton yarn (US sport); 100% mercerized cotton; approximately 112m (122 yd) per 50g/1³/₄oz ball

Jaeger Sienna
very lightweight cotton yarn (US fingering); 100% mercerized cotton; approximately 140m (153 yd) per 50g/1³/₄oz ball

Jaeger Silk
very lightweight silk yarn (US fingering); 100% silk; approximately 186m (203 yd) per 50g/1³/₄oz ball

GREAT PLAINS crewneck sweater

This design was my first for the Rowan Collection when I joined the Kaffe Fassett Studio. Taking the inspiration from a watercolour sketch of an American Indian woven basket, the original garment was knitted in Rowan Nice Cotton and Rowan Cotton Glacé, the palette reflected a warm sun-baked desert. For those who are a little daunted about taking on a multi-coloured project, this design is deceptively straight forward – just two colours per row all the way. In this new colourway, I wanted to create a handsome stoney palette, creating the mood of lichen corroded surfaces exposing layers of mineral, beautifully affected by the passage of time or when layers of rock pile on top of one another seen in quarry and cliff surfaces. The Rowan DK Tweed yarns lend themselves perfectly to this palette with speckles of colour caught in the tweed yarn giving an added texture to the design. Working with deep rich earthy tones in contrast with shades of dried sage, deep terracotta red, fresh periwinkle blue and cool touches of lavender.

Yarn

Rowan DK Tweed and Rowan Felted Tweed

One size to fit a range of sizes
To fit up to chest   138cm (54 in)

A	Rowan DK Tweed	green (866)	2 x 50g
B	Rowan DK Tweed	pale grey-green (851)	2 x 50g
C	Rowan DK Tweed	mid-blue (862)	2 x 50g
D	Rowan DK Tweed	rust (864)	2 x 50g
E	Rowan DK Tweed	oatmeal (850)	2 x 50g
F	Rowan DK Tweed	pale brown (853)	2 x 50g
G	Rowan DK Tweed	rose pink (861)	2 x 50g
H	Rowan Felted Tweed	rust (144)	1 x 50g
J	Rowan Felted Tweed	navy blue (133)	1 x 50g
L	Rowan Felted Tweed	pink-purple (139)	1 x 50g
M	Rowan Felted Tweed	green-blue (131)	1 x 50g
N	Rowan Felted Tweed	blue-grey (141)	1 x 50g
R	Rowan Felted Tweed	rose pink (137)	1 x 50g
S	Rowan Felted Tweed	green-gold (138)	1 x 50g

Needles

1 pair 3¼mm (no 10/US 3) needles
1 pair 4mm (no 8/US 6) needles
stitch holder

Tension

22 stitches and 28 rows to 10cm (4 in)
measured over patterned stocking
(stockinette) stitch using 4mm (no 8/US 6)
needles.

BACK

Using 3¼mm (no 10/US 3) needles, cast on
149 sts with yarn A.

Work rib

Work 25 rows in K1, P1 rib in stripe sequence
as folls and AT THE SAME TIME inc 6 sts
evenly across last row. 155 sts.
Work 1 row with yarn A.
Work 2 rows with yarn D.
Work 2 rows with yarn S.
Work 1 row with yarn H.
Work 2 rows with yarn E.
Work 2 rows with yarn G.
Work 1 row with yarn C.
Work 2 rows with yarn D.
Work 2 rows with yarn B.
Work 2 rows with yarn A.
Work 2 rows with yarn H.
Work 2 rows with yarn R.
Work 2 rows with yarn L.
Work 2 rows with yarn C.

Begin chart pattern

Change to 4mm (no 8/US 6) needles and yarn R.

Using the Fair Isle technique described in the basic information (see page 11), knitting in yarns as required, reading odd numbered K rows from right to left and even numbered P rows from left to right, beg with a K row, work in patt from back chart, which is worked entirely in st st, until chart row 136 has been completed, thus ending with a WS row.

Shape back neck

Divide for neck shaping on next row as folls:

Next row (RS): Work in patt until 59 sts on right-hand needle, turn, leaving rem sts on stitch holder.

Work each side of neck separately.

Next row: Keeping chart correct, cast off (bind off) 4 sts, work in patt to end. 55 sts.

Cast off (bind off) rem 55 sts.

With RS facing, rejoin yarn to rem sts on stitch holder, cast off (bind off) centre 37 sts for neckband, work in patt to end.

Complete to match first side, reversing shapings.

FRONT

Work as given for Back until chart row 116 has been completed, thus ending with a WS row.

Shape front neck

Divide for neck shaping on next row as folls:

Next row (RS): Work in patt until 72 sts on right-hand needle, turn, leaving rem sts on stitch holder.

Work each side of neck separately.

Cast off (bind off) 3 sts at beg of next row and 2 foll alt (other) rows. 63 sts.

Keeping chart correct, dec 1 st at neck edge on next 8 rows until 55 sts rem.

Cont without shaping until Front has same number of rows as Back to shoulder, thus ending with a WS row.

Cast off (bind off) rem 55 sts.

With RS facing, rejoin yarn to rem sts on stitch holder, slip centre 11 sts onto a stitch holder for neckband, work in patt to end.

Complete to match first side, reversing shapings.

SLEEVES (MAKE TWO)

Using 3¹/₄mm (no 10/US 3) needles, cast on 51 sts with yarn A.

Work rib as given for Back but inc 8 sts evenly across last row. 59 sts.

Begin chart pattern

Change to 4mm (no 8/US 6) needles and yarn R.

Using the Fair Isle technique described in the basic information (see page 11), knitting in yarns as required, reading odd numbered K rows from right to left and even numbered P rows from left to right, beg with a K row, work in patt from sleeve chart, which is worked entirely in st st, taking all inc sts into patt, inc 1 st at each end of 6th and every foll 4th row until 103 sts and chart row 90 has been completed.

Cast off (bind off) loosely and evenly.

FINISHING

Press all pieces on WS with a warm iron over a damp cloth. Join right shoulder seam using backstitch or mattress stitch.

Neckband

With RS facing, using 3¹/₄mm (no 10/US 3) needles with yarn A, pick up and K 27 sts down Left Front neck, 11 sts from stitch holder across Front neck, 27 sts up Right Front neck and 46 sts from stitch holder across Back neck. 111 sts.

Work 8 rows in K1, P1 rib in stripe sequence as folls:

Work 1 row with yarn A.

Work 2 rows with yarn B.

Work 1 row with yarn R.

Work 2 rows with yarn D.

Work 1 row with yarn L.

Work 1 row with yarn F.

Cast off (bind off) loosely and evenly in rib with yarn F.

Join left shoulder seam. Sew in sleeves using backstitch or mattress stitch, matching centre of sleeves to shoulder seam. Join side seams and sleeve seams using backstitch or mattress stitch. See the basic information (page 13) for further finishing instructions.

Key

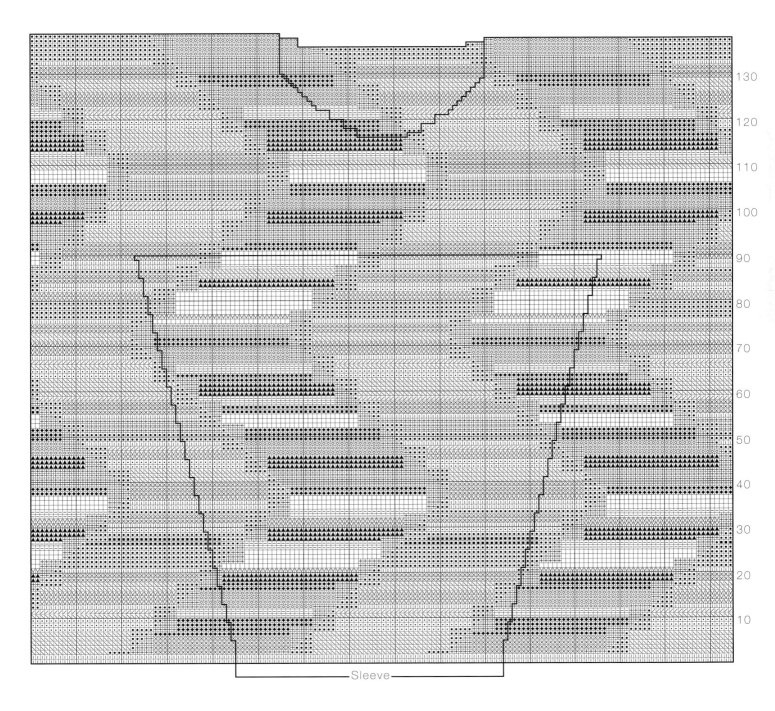

Sleeve

130

120

110

100

90

80

70

60

50

40

30

20

10

TALL POPPIES shawl-collared cardigan

Walking through the countryside in wild grasslands in the spring, you will inevitably find me dissolved over a splattering of red poppies blazing through grasses with their satisfyingly curved petals holding on to a willowy stem. In the United Kingdom, November 11 marks Remembrance Day in memory of the World Wars and, in commemoration, people sport paper red poppies in their buttonholes. The red spells passion, strength and depth. My imagination has longed to take the red oval shape with its black circular centre and repeat it throughout a whole design. I eventually satisfied my urge to play with the poppy motif by dotting these irregular flower shapes on this variegated, cool green, blue and purple background. I chose to finish the garment with a striped shawl collar and ribbing.

Yarn

Jaeger Matchmaker Merino 4 ply, Jaeger Matchmaker DK and Rowan True 4 ply Botany

One size to fit a range of sizes
To fit up to bust   117cm (46 in)

A	Jaeger Matchmaker Merino 4 ply	dark purple (706)	2 x 50g*
B	Jaeger Matchmaker Merino DK	fresh green (867)	3 x 50g
C	Jaeger Matchmaker Merino 4 ply	grey-blue (750)	4 x 50g*
D	Jaeger Matchmaker Merino 4 ply	apple green (713)	2 x 50g*
E	Jaeger Matchmaker Merino 4 ply	heather (701)	2 x 50g*
F	Jaeger Matchmaker Merino 4 ply	pale pink (694)	1 x 50g*
G	Jaeger Matchmaker Merino 4 Ply	orange (712)	1 x 50g*
H	Jaeger Matchmaker Merino 4 ply	red (697)	1 x 50g*
J	Jaeger Matchmaker Merino 4 ply	dark pink (633)	1 x 50g*
L	Jaeger Matchmaker Merino 4 ply	magenta (711)	1 x 50g*
M	Rowan True 4 ply Botany	violet (581)	1 x 50g*

All yarns marked with an * are to be worked double.

Needles

1 pair 3¼mm (no 10/US 3) needles
1 pair 4mm (no 8/US 6) needles
1 3¼mm (no 10/US 3) circular needle
stitch holder

Buttons

7

Tension

22 stitches and 30 rows to 10cm (4 in) measured over patterned stocking (stockinette) stitch using 4mm (no 8/US 6) needles.

BACK

Using 3¼mm (no 10/US 3) needles, cast on 132 sts with yarn E.

Work rib

Work 24 rows in K1, P1 rib in stripe sequence as folls:
Work 4 rows with yarn E.
Work 1 row with yarn D.
Work 3 rows with yarn E.
Work 2 rows with yarn D.
Work 2 rows with yarn E.
Work 6 rows with yarn D.
Work 1 row with yarn B.
Work 1 row with yarn D.
Work 2 rows with yarn B.
Work 2 rows with yarn D.

Begin chart pattern

Change to 4mm (no 8/US 6) needles.
Using the intarsia technique described in the basic information (see page 10), joining in and breaking off colours as required, reading odd numbered K rows from right to left and even numbered P rows from left to right, beg with a K row, work in patt from body chart, which is worked entirely in st st, until chart row 186 has been completed, thus ending with a WS row.

Shape back neck

Divide for neck shaping on next row as folls:
Next row: Work in patt until 51 sts on right-hand needle, turn, leaving rem sts on stitch holder.
Work each side of neck separately.
Next row: Cast off (bind off) 4 sts, work in patt to end.
Cont without shaping for 1 further row.
Cast off (bind off) rem 48 sts.
With RS facing, rejoin yarn to rem sts on stitch holder, cast off (bind off) centre 30 sts for neckband, work in patt to end.
Complete to match first side, reversing shapings.

LEFT FRONT

Using 3¼mm (no 10/US 3) needles, cast on 61 sts with yarn E.

Work rib

Work in rib as given for Back.

Begin chart pattern

Change to 4mm (no 8/US 6) needles.
Using the intarsia technique described in the basic information (see page 10), joining in and breaking off colours as required, reading odd numbered K rows from right to left and even numbered P rows from left to right, beg with a K row, work in patt from left front chart, which is worked entirely in st st, until chart row 110 has been completed, thus ending with a WS row.

Shape front neck

Dec 1 st at neck edge on next and every foll 5th row until 47 sts rem.
Cont without shaping until Left Front has same number of rows as Back to shoulder, thus ending with a WS row.
Cast off (bind off).

RIGHT FRONT

Work as given for Left Front but foll right front chart, reversing all shapings.

SLEEVES (MAKE TWO)

Using 3¼mm (no 10/US 3) needles, cast on 56 sts with yarn E.

Work rib

Work 16 rows in rib as given for Back.

Begin chart pattern

Change to 4mm (no 8/US 6) needles.

Using the intarsia technique described in the basic information (see page 10), joining in and breaking off colours as required, reading odd numbered K rows from right to left and even numbered P rows from left to right, beg with a K row, work in patt from sleeve chart, which is worked entirely in st st, taking all inc sts into patt, inc 1 st at each end of 6th and every foll 5th row until 110 sts.

Keeping chart correct, cont without shaping for 4 further rows.

Cast off (bind off) loosely and evenly.

FINISHING

Press all pieces on WS with a warm iron over a damp cloth. Join both shoulder seams using backstitch or mattress stitch.

Collar and front bands (worked in one piece)

With RS facing, using 3¼mm (no 10/US 3) circular needle with yarn E, pick up and K 96 sts up Right Front to beg of neck shaping, 58 sts up Right Front neck, 46 sts across Back neck, 58 sts down Left Front neck, and 96 sts down Left Front. 354 sts.

Work 3 rows in K1, P1 rib foll stripe sequence as given for Back.

Make buttonholes

1st buttonhole row: Work 4 sts in K1, P1 rib, * cast off (bind off) 2 sts in K1, P1 rib, work 13 sts in K1, P1 rib, rep from * 5 times, cast off (bind off) 2 sts in K1, P1 rib, work in K1, P1 rib to end.

2nd buttonhole row: Work in K1, P1 rib across all sts casting on 2 sts over those cast off (bound off) on previous row.

Cont in K1, P1 rib foll stripe sequence as given for Back.

Next row: Work in K1, P1 rib until 258 sts on right-hand needle, wrap st, turn.

Next row: Work in K1, P1 rib until 152 sts on right-hand needle, wrap st, turn.

Next row: Work in K1, P1 rib until 151 sts on right-hand needle, wrap st, turn.

Next row: Work in K1, P1 rib until 150 sts on right-hand needle, wrap st, turn.

Cont shaping collar as set until 33 rows have been worked at back neck.

Next row: Work in K1, P1 across all sts picking up loops from wrap sts and knitting together.

Cast off (bind off) loosely and evenly in rib.

Sew in sleeves using backstitch or mattress stitch, matching centre of sleeves to shoulder seam. Join side seams and sleeve seams using backstitch or mattress stitch. Sew buttons on to correspond with buttonholes.

See the basic information (page 13) for further finishing instructions.

Key

- A
- B
- C
- D
- E
- F
- G
- H
- J
- L
- M

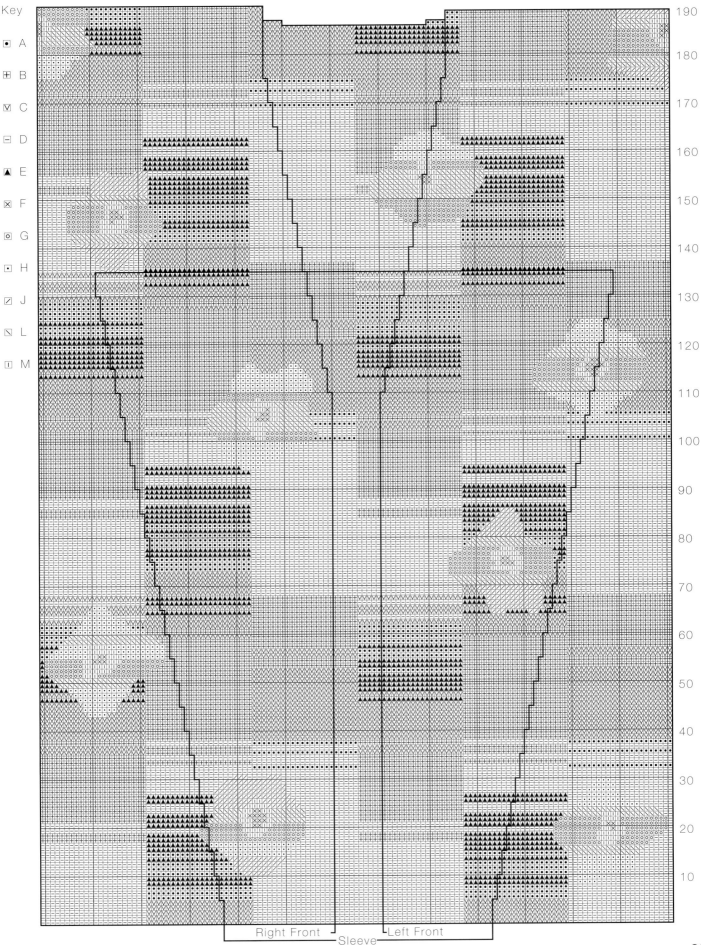

Right Front — Sleeve — Left Front

NOMAD v-neck cardigan

On a trip to Syria I had the opportunity to visit a Nomad family in the desert. Their weather-beaten canvas tent was lined completely with homemade crazy patchwork and the dirt floor was a collage of woven blankets and rugs, creating a festive, welcoming interior amidst the bleak surroundings. The interior of the tent was so different from what we see in the West. I have tried to capture the daringly outlandish mix of colours in this garment and their layout is based on a kilim carpet.

Yarn

Rowan Wool Cotton and Rowan Handknit DK

One size to fit a range of sizes
To fit up to bust   132cm (52 in)

A	Rowan Wool Cotton	olive green (907)	2 x 50g
B	Rowan Wool Cotton	sage green (930)	1 x 50g
C	Rowan Handknit DK	artichoke (209)	2 x 50g
D	Rowan Handknit DK	lime green (219)	2 x 50g
E	Rowan Handknit DK	mustard (229)	2 x 50g
F	Rowan Handknit DK	blue-green (228)	2 x 50g
G	Rowan Handknit DK	natural (205)	1 x 50g
H	Rowan Wool Cotton	forest green (906)	3 x 50g
J	Rowan Wool Cotton	blue-grey (905)	2 x 50g
L	Rowan Wool Cotton	mulberry (931)	2 x 50g
M	Rowan Wool Cotton	dusky pink (902)	2 x 50g
N	Rowan Wool Cotton	dark red (911)	2 x 50g
P	Rowan Handknit DK	scarlet red (215)	2 x 50g

Needles

1 pair 3¼mm (no 10/US 3) needles
1 pair 4mm (no 8/US 6) needles
1 3¼mm (no 10/US 3) circular needle
stitch holder

Buttons

5

Tension

20 stitches and 28 rows to 10cm (4 in) measured over patterned stocking (stockinette) stitch using 4mm (no 8/US 6) needles.

BACK

Using 3¼mm (no 10/US 3) needles, cast on 134 sts with yarn H.

Work rib

Work 17 rows in K1, P1 rib in stripe sequence as folls:
Work 2 rows with yarn H.
Work 1 row with yarn J.
Work 1 row with yarn F.
Work 1 row with yarn G.
Work 1 row with yarn D.
Work 1 row with yarn E.
Work 1 row with yarn C.
Work 1 row with yarn L.
Work 1 row with yarn M.
Work 1 row with yarn H.
Work 1 row with yarn J.
Work 1 row with yarn F.
Work 1 row with yarn D.
Work 1 row with yarn C.
Work 1 row with yarn E.
Work 1 row with yarn G.

Begin chart pattern

Change to 4mm (no 8/US 6) needles.
Using the intarsia technique described in the basic information (see page 10), joining in and breaking off colours as required, reading odd numbered K rows from right to left and even numbered P rows from left to right, beg with a K row, work in patt from body chart, which is worked entirely in st st, until chart row 148 has been completed, thus ending with a WS row.

Shape back neck

Divide for neck shaping on next row as folls:
Next row (RS): Work in patt until 49 sts on right-hand needle, turn, leaving rem sts on stitch holder.
Cont without shaping for 1 further row.
Cast off (bind off) rem 49 sts.
With RS facing, rejoin yarn to rem sts on stitch holder, cast off (bind off) centre 36 sts for neckband, work in patt to end.
Complete to match first side, reversing shapings.

LEFT FRONT

Using 3¼mm (no 10/US 3) needles, cast on 64 sts with yarn H.

Work rib

Work in rib as given for Back.

Begin chart pattern

Change to 4mm (no 8/US 6) needles.
Using the intarsia technique described in the basic information (see page 10), joining in and breaking off colours as required, reading odd numbered K rows from right to left and even numbered P rows from left to right, beg with a K row, work in patt from left front chart, which is worked entirely in st st, until chart row 91 has been completed, thus ending with a RS row.

Shape front neck

Keeping chart correct, dec 1 st at neck edge on next and every foll 4th row until 49 sts rem.
Cont without shaping until Left Front has the same number of rows as Back to shoulder, thus ending with a WS row.
Cast off (bind off) rem 49 sts.

RIGHT FRONT

Work as given for Left Front but foll right front chart, reversing all shapings.

SLEEVES (MAKE TWO)

Using 3¼mm (no 10/US 3) needles, cast on 48 sts with yarn H.

Work rib

Work rib as given for Back.

Begin chart pattern

Change to 4mm (no 8/US 6) needles.

Using the intarsia technique described in the basic information (see page 10), joining in and breaking off colours as required, reading odd numbered K rows from right to left and even numbered P rows from left to right, beg with a K row, work in patt from sleeve chart, which is worked entirely in st st, taking all inc sts into patt, inc 1 st at each end of 5th and then every foll 4th row until 90 sts.

Keeping chart correct, cont without shaping for 6 further rows.

Cast off (bind off) loosely and evenly.

FINISHING

Press all pieces on WS with a warm iron over a damp cloth. Join both shoulder seams using backstitch or mattress stitch.

Collar and front bands (worked as one piece)

With RS facing, using 3¼mm (no 10/US 3) circular needle with yarn H, pick up and K 93 sts up Right Front to beg of neck shaping, 60 sts up Right Front neck, 40 sts across Back neck, 60 sts down Left Front neck, and 93 sts down Left Front. 346 sts.

Work 3 rows in K1, P1 rib foll stripe sequence as given for Back.

Make buttonholes

1st buttonhole row: Keeping stripe sequence correct, work 3 sts in rib, * cast off (bind off) 2 sts in rib, work in rib until 20 sts on right-hand needle after last cast-off (bind-off) including stitch used in last cast-off (bind-off), rep from * 3 times, cast off (bind off) 2 sts in rib, work in rib to end.

2nd buttonhole row: Keeping stripe sequence correct, work in K1, P1 rib as set across all sts casting on 2 sts over those cast off (bound off) on previous row.

Keeping stripe sequence correct, cont in K1, P1 rib for 2 further rows.

Change to yarn L only.

Cast off (bind off) loosely and evenly in rib.

Sew in sleeves using backstitch or mattress stitch, matching centre of sleeves to shoulder seam. Join side seams and sleeve seams using backstitch or mattress stitch. Sew buttons on to correspond with buttonholes. See the basic information (page 13) for further finishing instructions.

Key

◉ A   ⊟ D   ◙ G   ◩ L   ◤ R

⊞ B   ▲ E   ⊡ H   ⊡ M

☑ C   ☒ F   ◪ J   ◼ N

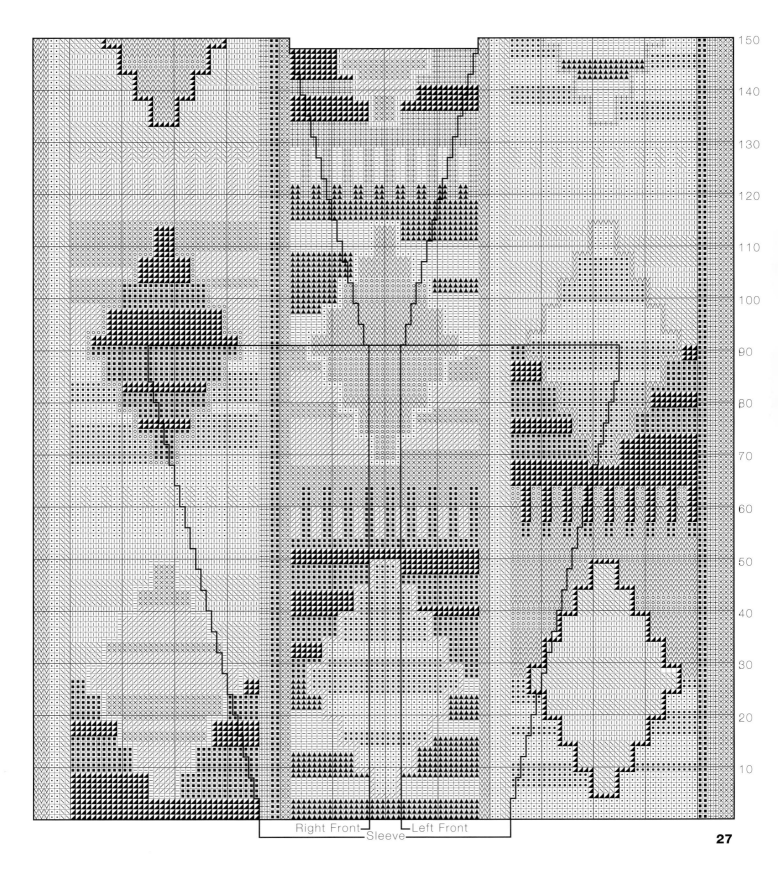

Right Front — Sleeve — Left Front

SEASCAPE crewneck sweater

My eyes are always out on stalks for a good design idea. Travelling on a train one day, I spotted a fellow passenger's bag, which was made from a kilim carpet in shades of burnt umber, baked red, blues and brown. The design comprised wide, flattened diamond windows separated by a stepped border and it was this that informed the pattern of this sweater. I am constantly drawn by the power of the ocean, particularly where there are great tidal ranges and varying storms. Consequently, this design also reminds me of the Welsh coast where I was brought up. Taking shades of blue, rust and red with lavender for the lattice, I have tried to capture the emotion and atmosphere of the sea in the colouring for this design.

Yarn

Rowan DK Tweed, Rowan Felted Tweed, Rowan True 4 ply Botany and Rowan Wool Cotton

One size to fit a range of sizes
To fit up to chest   122cm (48 in)

A	Rowan DK Tweed	rose pink (861)	4 x 50g
B	Rowan DK Tweed	rust (864)	2 x 50g
C	Rowan Felted Tweed	blue-grey (141)	2 x 50g
D	Rowan Felted Tweed	russett red (144)	2 x 50g
E	Rowan Felted Tweed	burgundy (134)	2 x 50g
F	Rowan DK Tweed	mid-blue (862)	3 x 50g
G	Rowan True 4 ply Botany	dark red (549)	3 x 50g*
H	Rowan Wool Cotton	sky blue (934)	2 x 50g
J	Rowan Felted Tweed	pink-purple (139)	2 x 50g

Yarn marked with an * is to be worked double.

Needles

1 pair 3¼mm (no 10/US 3) needles
1 pair 4mm (no 8/US 6) needles
stitch holder

Tension

22 stitches and 29 rows to 10cm (4 in) measured over patterned stocking (stockinette) stitch using 4mm (no 8/US 6) needles.

BACK

Using 3¼mm (no 10/US 3) needles, cast on 134 sts with yarn D.

Work rib

Work 12 rows in K1, P1 rib in stripe sequence as folls:
Work 2 rows with yarn D.
Work 2 rows with yarn F.
Work 2 rows with yarn G.
Work 2 rows with yarn E.
Work 2 rows with yarn A.
Work 1 row with yarn H.
Work 1 row with yarn B.
Rep last 12 rows 1 further time, thus ending with a WS row.

Begin chart pattern

Change to 4mm (no 8/US 6) needles.
Using the intarsia technique described in the basic information (see page 10), joining in and breaking off colours as required, reading odd numbered K rows from right to left and even numbered P rows from left to right, beg with a K row, work in patt from body chart, which is worked entirely in st st, until chart row 172 has been completed, thus ending with a WS row.

Shape back neck

Divide for neck shaping on next row as folls:
Next row (RS): Work in patt until 48 sts on right-hand needle, turn, leaving rem sts on stitch holder.
Work each side of neck separately.
Next row: Keeping chart correct, cast off (bind off) 2 sts, work in patt to end.
Cast off (bind off) rem 46 sts.
With RS facing, rejoin yarn to rem sts on stitch holder, cast off (bind off) centre 36 sts for neckband, work in patt to end.
Complete to match first side, reversing shapings.

FRONT

Work as given for Back until chart row 150 has been completed, thus ending with a WS row.

Shape front neck

Divide for neck shaping on next row as folls:
Next row: Work in patt until 59 sts on right-hand needle, turn, leaving rem sts on stitch holder.
Work each side of neck separately.
Keeping chart correct, dec 1 st at neck edge on next 13 rows until 46 sts rem.
Cont without shaping until Front has same number of rows as Back to shoulder, thus ending with a WS row.
Cast off (bind off) rem 46 sts.
With RS facing, rejoin yarn to rem sts on stitch holder, slip centre 16 sts onto a stitch holder for neckband, work in patt to end.
Complete to match first side, reversing shapings.

SLEEVES (MAKE TWO)

Using 3¼mm (no 10/US 3) needles, cast on 56 sts with yarn D.

Work rib

Work rib as given for Back.

Begin chart pattern

Change to 4mm (no 8/US 6) needles.
Using the intarsia technique described in the basic information (see page 10), joining in and breaking off colours as required, reading odd numbered K rows from right to left and even numbered P rows from left to right, beg with a K row, work in patt from sleeve chart, which is worked entirely in st st, taking all inc sts into patt, inc 1 st at each end of 5th and

SEASCAPE crewneck sweater

then every foll 4th row until there are 112 sts.
Cont without shaping for 9 further rows.
Cast off (bind off) loosely and evenly.

FINISHING

Press all pieces on WS with a warm iron over
a damp cloth. Join right shoulder seam using
backstitch or mattress stitch.

Neckband

With RS facing, using 3¼mm (no 10/US 3)
needles with yarn A, pick up and K 21 sts
down Left Front neck, 16 sts from stitch
holder across Front neck, 21 sts up Right
Front neck and 40 sts from stitch holder
across Back neck. 98 sts.

Work 10 rows in K1, P1 rib in stripe
sequence as folls:
Work 2 rows with yarn A.
Work 2 rows with yarn E.
Work 2 rows with yarn G.
Work 2 rows with yarn F.
Work 2 rows with yarn D.
Cast off (bind off) loosely and evenly in rib.
Join left shoulder seam using backstitch or
mattress stitch. Sew in sleeves using
backstitch or mattress stitch, matching centre
of sleeves to shoulder seam. Join side seams
and sleeve seams using backstitch or
mattress stitch. See the basic information
(page 13) for further finishing instructions.

Key

- ⊡ A
- ⊞ B
- ☑ C
- ⊟ D
- ▲ E
- ⊠ F
- ⊡ G
- ⊡ H
- ☑ J
- ◩ L
- ⊡ M

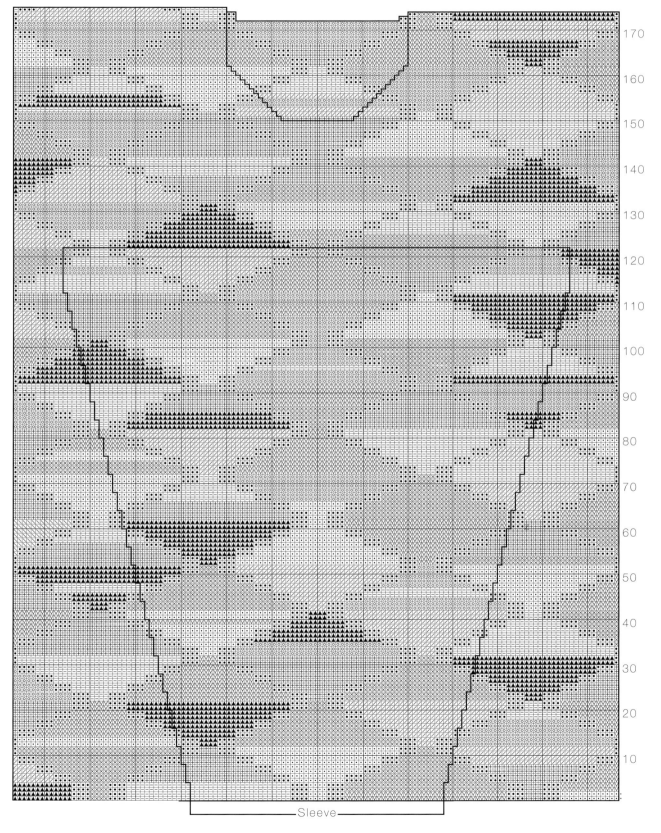

Sleeve

TIE DYE shawl-collared cardigan

When I look at this finished garment, split pomegranates, crushed red berries and Captain Cook's treasure of emeralds, sapphires and rubies are conjured up in my mind. Recent travels have taken me to India. I left with a half-empty backpack and returned with it bulging with articles from the textile market in Ajuna, Goa. When I was there I saw fields and roads lined with colourful glistening textiles and handcrafts, bold patterned bedspreads flapping in the sea breeze and bags and clothing encrusted with mirror sequins hanging from string and wooden structures. It was hard not to be seduced by the impact of these vivid hues. As a result, I wanted to make a garment that captured the jewel-like depth of the saturated colours, which I hope I have caught in Tie Dye.

Yarn

Jaeger Alpaca, Rowan Felted Tweed, Rowan DK Tweed, Rowan Wool Cotton, Rowan Cotton Glacé, Rowan 4 ply Cotton and Jaeger Matchmaker Merino 4 ply

One size to fit a range of sizes
To fit up to bust   112cm (44 in)

A	Jaeger Alpaca	crimson red (388)	5 x 50g*
B	Rowan Felted Tweed	russett red (144)	5 x 50g
C	Rowan DK Tweed	rust (864)	2 x 50g
D	Rowan Wool Cotton	red (911)	2 x 50g
E	Rowan Cotton Glacé	dark red	2 x 50g
F	Rowan Wool Cotton	green-yellow	1 x 50g
G	Rowan DK Tweed	gold	1 x 50g
H	Rowan Wool Cotton	mid blue	1 x 50g
J	Rowan Felted Tweed	navy blue	1 x 50g
L	Rowan 4 ply Cotton	orange	1 x 50g*
M	Jaeger Matchmaker Merino 4 ply	beige	1 x 50g*

All yarns marked with an * are to be worked double.

Needles

1 pair 3¼mm (no 10/US 3) needles
1 pair 4mm (no 8/US 6) needles
stitch holder

Buttons

6

Tension

21 stitches and 29 rows to 10cm (4 in) measured over patterned stocking (stockinette) stitch using 4mm (no 8/US 6) needles.

BACK

Using 3¼mm (no 10/US 3) needles, cast on 118 sts with yarn A.

Work hem

Change to yarn B.
Work 10 rows in moss st (seed st), thus ending with a WS row.

Begin chart pattern

Change to 4mm (no 8/US 6) needles and yarn A.
Using the Fair Isle technique described in the basic information (see page 11), knitting in yarns as required, reading odd numbered K rows from right to left and even numbered P rows from left to right, beg with a K row, work in patt from body chart, which is worked entirely in st st, until chart row 116 has been completed but AT THE SAME TIME foll stripe sequence for background as folls:
Work 4 rows with yarn A.
Work 2 rows with yarn E.
Work 2 rows with yarn C.
Work 3 rows with yarn A.
Work 2 rows with yarn B.

Work 3 rows with yarn D.
Work 1 row with yarn C.
Work 3 rows with yarn E.
Work 1 row with yarn D.
Work 2 rows with yarn B.
Work 4 rows with yarn A.
Work 2 rows with yarn B.
Work 3 rows with yarn D.
Work 3 rows with yarn A.
Work 1 row with yarn E.
Work 2 rows with yarn B.
Work 2 rows with yarn C.
Rep stripe sequence throughout chart.

Shape armholes

Cast off (bind off) 4 sts at beg of next 2 rows. 110 sts.
Dec 1 st at each end on next 6 rows. 98 sts.
Cont without shaping until chart row 176 has been worked, thus ending with a WS row.

Shape back neck

Divide for neck shaping on next row as folls:
Next row (RS): Work in patt until 33 sts on right-hand needle, turn, leaving rem sts on stitch holder.

Work each side of neck separately.
Next row: Cast off (bind off) 3 sts, work in patt to end. 30 sts.
Cont without shaping for 2 further rows.
Cast off (bind off) rem 30 sts.
With RS facing, rejoin yarn to rem sts, cast off (bind off) centre 32 sts for neckband, work in patt to end.
Complete to match first side, reversing shapings.

LEFT FRONT

Using 3¼mm (no 10/US 3) needles, cast on 54 sts with yarn A.

Work hem

Change to yarn B.
Work 10 rows in moss st (seed st), thus ending with a WS row.

Begin chart pattern

Change to 4mm (no 8/US 6) needles and yarn A.
Using the Fair Isle technique described in the basic information (see page 11), knitting in yarns as required, reading odd numbered K

rows from right to left and even numbered P rows from left to right, beg with a K row, work in patt from left front chart, which is worked entirely in st st, until chart row 116 has been completed but AT THE SAME TIME foll stripe sequence for background as given for Back.

Shape armholes

Next row (RS): Cast off (bind off) 4 sts, work in patt to end. 50 sts.

Cont without shaping for 1 further row.

Dec 1 st at armhole edge on next 6 rows. 44 sts.

Cont without shaping until chart row 157 has been worked, thus ending with a RS row.

Shape neck

Cast off (bind off) 5 sts at beg of next row and 2 sts at beg of next alt (other) row. 37 sts.

Dec 1 st at neck edge on next 7 rows. 30 sts.

Cont without shaping until Front has same numbers of rows as Back to shoulder.

Cast off (bind off) rem 30 sts.

RIGHT FRONT

Work as given for Left Front, reversing all shapings.

SLEEVES (MAKE TWO)

Using 3¹/₄mm (no 10/US 3) needles, cast on 48 sts with yarn A.

Work cuff

Change to yarn B.

Work 10 rows in moss st (seed st), thus ending with a WS row.

Begin chart pattern

Change to 4mm (no 8/US 6) needles and yarn A.

Using the Fair Isle technique described in the basic information (see page 11), knitting in yarns as required, reading odd numbered K rows from right to left and even numbered P rows from left to right, beg with a K row, work in patt from sleeve chart, which is worked entirely in st st, and AT THE SAME TIME foll stripe sequence as given for Back, taking all inc sts into patt, inc 1 st at each end of 6th row and every foll 5th row until 96 sts.

Cont without shaping until chart row 122 has been completed, thus ending with a WS row.

Shape armholes

Cast off (bind off) 4 sts at beg of next 2 rows. 88 sts.

Dec 1 st each end of next 6 rows. 76 sts.

Cast off (bind off) rem 76 sts.

FINISHING

Press all pieces on WS with a warm iron over a damp cloth.

Button band

With RS facing, using 3¹/₄mm (no 10/US 3) needles with yarn B, pick up and K 133 sts evenly along Left Front opening edge.

Row 1: K1 with yarn A (to match bottom edge of hem), work in moss st (seed st) to end with yarn B.

Row 2: Work in moss st (seed st) to last st with yarn B, K1 with yarn A.

Rep last 2 rows 4 further times.

Change to yarn A only.

Work 1 row in moss st (seed st) as set.

Cast off (bind off) with yarn A.

Buttonhole band

With RS facing, using 3¹/₄mm (no 10/US 3) needles with yarn B, pick up and K 133 sts evenly along Right Front opening edge.

Row 1: Work in moss st (seed st) to last st with yarn B, K1 with yarn A (to match bottom edge of hem).

Row 2: K1 with yarn A, work in moss st (seed st) to end with yarn B.

Rep row 1 again.

Make buttonholes

1st buttonhole row: Work 5 sts in moss st (seed st), yfwd, K2tog, * work 22 sts in moss st (seed st), yfwd, K2tog, rep from * to last 6 sts, work 6 sts in moss st (seed st).

2nd buttonhole row:

Work 5 further rows in moss st (seed st) as set.

Change to yarn A only.

Work 1 row in moss st (seed st) as set.

Cast off (bind off) with yarn A.

Join shoulder seams using backstitch or mattress stitch.

Collar

With RS facing, using 3¹/₄mm (no 10/US 3) needles with yarn B, starting half way across top of buttonhole band pick up and K 33 sts up Right Front neck, 43 sts across Back neck, 33 sts down Left Front neck finishing half way across top of button band. 109 sts.

Work in moss st (seed st) until collar measures 8cm (3 in), thus ending with a WS row.

Change to yarn A.

Work 1 row in moss st (seed st) as set.

Cast off (bind off).

Sew in sleeves using backstitch or mattress stitch, matching centre of sleeves to shoulder seam. Join side seams and sleeve seams using backstitch or mattress stitch. Sew on buttons to correspond with buttonholes. See the basic information (page 13) for further finishing instructions.

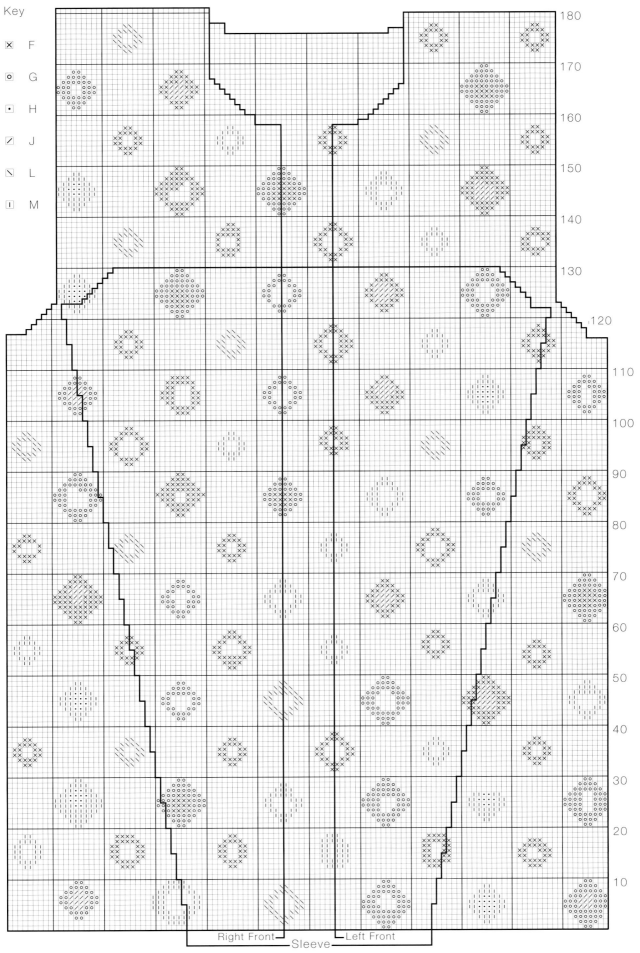

Key

× F

o G

· H

⊠ J

⊠ L

⊡ M

Right Front — Sleeve — Left Front

35

LADYBIRD v-neck waistcoat

There is something about African body painting that is quite riveting with its refreshing sense of confidence that results in perfect placement and markings. In a book called *Decorated Skin* there is a native man from South America painted with large red spots on a white powder base. The power of these offset circles randomly placed like the markings of a wild cat translated so easily into a knitwear design. Daringly, I have used a vibrant red cashmere yarn on an olive green background. This design is open to so many possibilities for changing its colours. How about violet on a rich inky blue or fresh white on black? The choice is yours.

Yarn

Jaeger Matchmaker Merino 4 ply and Jaeger Cashmere

One size to fit a range of sizes
To fit up to chest   112cm (44 in)

A	Jaeger Matchmaker Merino 4 ply	olive green (723)	4 x 50g
B	Jaeger Cashmere	red (107)	3 x 25g

Needles

1 pair 2³/₄mm (no 12/US 1) needles
1 pair 3¹/₄mm (no 10/US 3) needles
1 2³/₄mm (no 12/US 1) circular needle
stitch holder

Buttons

5

Tension

27 stitches and 36 rows to 10cm (4 in) measured over patterned stocking (stockinette) stitch using 3¹/₄mm (no 10/US 3) needles.

BACK

Using 2³/₄mm (no 12/US 1) needles, cast on 148 sts with yarn B.

Work rib

Work 1 row in K1, P1 rib.
Change to yarn A.
Work 13 further rows in rib as set.

Begin chart pattern

Change to 3¹/₄mm (no 10/US 3) needles.
Using the Fair Isle technique described in the basic information (see page 11), knitting in yarns as required, reading odd numbered K rows from right to left and even numbered P rows from left to right, beg with a K row, work in patt from back chart, which is worked entirely in st st, until chart row 126 has been completed, thus ending with a WS row.

Shape armholes

Keeping chart correct, cast off (bind off) 4 sts at beg of next 2 rows and 3 sts at beg of foll 2 rows. 134 sts.
Dec 1 st each end of next 17 rows. 100 sts.
Cont without shaping until chart row 202 has been completed, thus ending with a WS row.

Shape back neck

Divide for neck shaping on next row as folls:
Next row (RS): Work in patt until 30 sts on right-hand needle, turn, leaving rem sts on stitch holder.
Work each side of neck separately.
Next row: Cast off (bind off) 4 sts, work in patt to end.

Cast off (bind off) rem 26 sts.
With RS facing, rejoin yarn to rem sts on stitch holder, cast off (bind off) centre 40 sts for neckband, work in patt to end.
Complete to match first side, reversing shapings.

LEFT FRONT

Using 2³/₄mm (no 12/US 1) needles, cast on 72 sts with yarn B.

Work rib

Work rib as given for Back.

Begin chart pattern

Change to 3¹/₄mm (no 10/US 3) needles.
Using the Fair Isle technique described in the basic information (see page 11), knitting in yarns as required, reading odd numbered K rows from right to left and even numbered P rows from left to right, beg with a K row, work in patt from left front chart, which is worked entirely in st st, until chart row 116 has been completed, thus ending with a WS row.

Shape front neck and armhole

Keeping chart correct, dec 1 st at neck edge on next and every foll 4th row and AT THE SAME TIME cast off (bind off) 4 sts at armhole edge on foll 10th row and 3 sts on foll 12th row then dec 1 st at armhole edge on foll alt (other) row and foll 16 rows. 40 sts.
Cont neck shaping as set until 26 sts rem.
Cont without shaping until Left Front has

same number of rows as Back to shoulder, thus ending with a WS row.
Cast off (bind off).

RIGHT FRONT

Work as given for Left Front but foll right front chart, reversing all shapings.

FINISHING

Press all pieces on WS with a warm iron over a damp cloth. Join both shoulder seams using backstitch or mattress stitch.

Neck and front bands (worked in one piece)

With RS facing, using 2³/₄mm (no 12/US 1) circular needle with yarn A, pick up and K 102 sts up Right Front to beg of neck shaping, 76 sts up Right Front neck, 56 sts across Back neck, 76 sts down Left Front neck, and 102 sts down Left Front from beg of neck shaping. 412 sts.
Work 3 rows in K1, P1 rib, working first and last st with yarn B to match bottom edge of rib and the remainder with yarn A.

Make buttonholes

1st buttonhole row: Work 4 sts in rib, * cast off (bind off) 2 sts in rib, work in rib until 22 sts on right-hand needle after last cast-off (bind-off) including stitch used in last cast-off (bind-off), rep from * 3 times, cast off (bind off) 2 sts in rib, work in rib to end.

2nd buttonhole row: Work in rib as set

LADYBIRD v-neck waistcoat

Key

☐ A

⦿ B

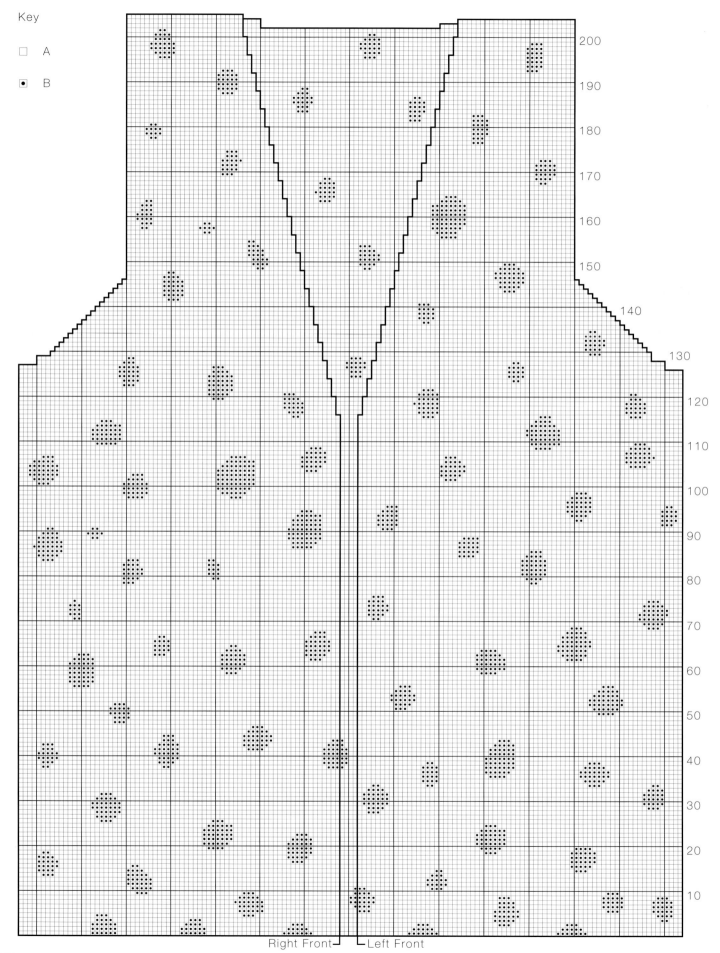

Right Front — — Left Front

200
190
180
170
160
150
140
130
120
110
100
90
80
70
60
50
40
30
20
10

across all sts casting on 2 sts over those cast off (bound off) on previous row.
Work a further 2 rows in rib as set.
Change to yarn B.
Work 1 further row in rib as set.
Cast off (bind off) loosely and evenly in rib.

Armhole bands

With RS facing, using 2³⁄₄mm (no 12/US 1) needles with yarn A, pick up and K 124 sts evenly around armhole edge.
Work 6 rows in K1, P1 rib.
Change to yarn B.
Work 1 further row in rib as set.
Cast off (bind off) loosely and evenly in rib.
Join side seams using mattress stitch. Sew buttons on to correspond with buttonholes.
See the basic information (page 13) for further finishing instructions.

JAZZY v-neck waistcoat

The palette of this garment reminds me of the freshness Picasso caught in some of his paintings, but it was primarily inspired by an antique, intricately woven Kurdish wedding pillow that Kaffe once bought me. The original colours were rather subdued so this is my upscale version of the design with vibrating colours. I originally knitted the design with a dusty pink lattice but I felt it didn't give the waistcoat the snappiness I was looking for. Now the fiery chilli pepper red gives the design the perfect kick. This waistcoat looks great on both sexes; the longer length pictured is most flattering for women whilst a shortened box waistcoat would sparkle under a man's blazer. Although it looks challenging to knit, each diamond, in fact, uses only two colours per row.

Yarn
Rowan Cotton Glacé

One size to fit a range of sizes
To fit up to bust/chest   112cm (44 in)

A	Rowan Cotton Glacé	red (741)	4 x 50g
B	Rowan Cotton Glacé	gold (802)	1 x 50g
C	Rowan Cotton Glacé	turquoise (801)	1 x 50g
D	Rowan Cotton Glacé	blue-green (797)	1 x 50g
E	Rowan Cotton Glacé	dusky plum (793)	1 x 50g
F	Rowan Cotton Glacé	navy blue (746)	1 x 50g
G	Rowan Cotton Glacé	olive green (739)	1 x 50g
H	Rowan Cotton Glacé	pale green (800)	1 x 50g
J	Rowan Cotton Glacé	lavender (787)	1 x 50g
L	Rowan Cotton Glacé	rose pink (724)	1 x 50g
M	Rowan Cotton Glacé	dark rust (445)	1 x 50g
N	Rowan Cotton Glacé	terracotta (786)	1 x 50g
R	Rowan Cotton Glacé	sage green (780)	1 x 50g

Needles
1 pair 3mm (no 11/US 2–3) needles
1 pair 3¼mm (no 10/US 3) needles
1 3mm (no 11/US 2–3) circular needle
stitch holder

Buttons
7

Tension
23 stitches and 32 rows to 10cm (4 in) measured over patterned stocking (stockinette) stitch using 3¼mm (no 10/US 3) needles.

BACK
Using 3mm (no 11/US 2–3) needles, cast on 138 sts with yarn L.

Work rib
Work 2 rows in K2, P2 rib.
Change to yarn A.
Work 14 further rows in rib as set.

Begin chart pattern
Change to 3¼mm (no 10/US 3) needles.
Using the intarsia technique described in the basic information (see page 10), joining in and breaking off colours as required, reading odd numbered K rows from right to left and even numbered P rows from left to right, beg with a K row, work in patt from body chart, which is worked mainly in st st until, chart row 144 has been completed, thus ending with a WS row.

Shape armholes
Keeping chart correct, cast off (bind off) 4 sts at beg of next 2 rows and 2 sts at beg of foll 2 rows. 126 sts.
Dec 1 st at each end of next 8 rows. 110 sts.

Cont in patt until chart row 224 has been worked, thus ending with a WS row.

Shape back neck
Divide for neck shaping on next row as folls:

Next row: Work in patt until 37 sts on right-hand needle, turn, leaving rem sts on stitch holder, work in patt to end.
Cont without shaping for 1 further row.
Cast off (bind off) rem 37 sts.
With RS facing, rejoin yarn to rem sts on stitch holder, cast off (bind off) centre 36 sts for neckband, work in patt to end.
Complete to match first side, reversing shapings.

LEFT FRONT
Using 3mm (no 11/US 2–3) needles, cast on 67 sts with yarn A.

Work rib
Work rib as given for Back.

Begin chart pattern
Change to 3¼mm (no 10/US 3) needles.
Using the intarsia technique described in the basic information (see page 10), joining in and breaking off colours as required, reading odd numbered K rows from right to left and even numbered P rows from left to right, beg with a K row, work in patt from left front chart, which is worked mainly in st st until, chart row 135 has been completed, thus ending with a RS row.

Shape front neck and armholes
Keeping chart correct, dec 1 st at neck edge on next and every foll 7th row 5 times then every 5th row 10 times and AT THE SAME TIME cast off (bind off) 4 sts at armhole edge on chart row 145 and 2 sts on foll alt (other) row then dec 1 st at armhole edge on foll 8 rows. 36 sts.
Cont without shaping until Left Front has same number of rows as Back to shoulder, thus ending with a WS row.
Cast off (bind off).

RIGHT FRONT
Work as given for Left Front but foll right front chart, reversing all shapings.

JAZZY v-neck waistcoat

FINISHING

Press all pieces on WS with a warm iron over a damp cloth. Join both shoulder seams using backstitch or mattress stitch.

Neck and front bands (worked in one piece)

With RS facing, using 3mm (no 11/US 2–3) circular needle with yarn A, pick up and K 142 sts from bottom of Right Front up to beg of neck shaping, 64 sts up Right Front neck, 40 sts across Back neck, 64 sts down Left Front neck, 142 sts down Left Front to bottom edge. 452 sts.

Work 3 rows in K2, P2 rib.

Make buttonholes

1st buttonhole row: Work 4 sts in rib, * cast off (bind off) 2 sts in rib, work 22 sts in rib, rep from * 6 times, cast off (bind off) 2 sts in rib, work in rib to end.

2nd buttonhole row: Work in rib as set casting on 2 sts over those cast off (bound off) on previous row.

Work 2 further rows in rib.

Change to yarn L.

Work 2 further rows in rib.

Cast off (bind off) loosely and evenly in rib.

Armhole bands

With RS facing, using 3mm (no 11/US 2–3) needles with yarn A, pick up and K 124 sts evenly around armhole edge.

Work 4 rows in K2, p2 rib.

Change to yarn L.

Work 2 further rows in rib as set.

Cast off (bind off) loosely and evenly in rib. Join side seams using backstitch or mattress stitch. Sew buttons on to correspond with buttonholes. See the basic information (page 13) for further finishing instructions.

The shortened box waistcoat pictured above looks great on men whilst the longer-length waistcoat below is most flattering for women.

Key

- A
+ B
v C
- D
▲ E
× F
o G
· H
⁄ J
＼ L
⊡ M
■ N
◢ R

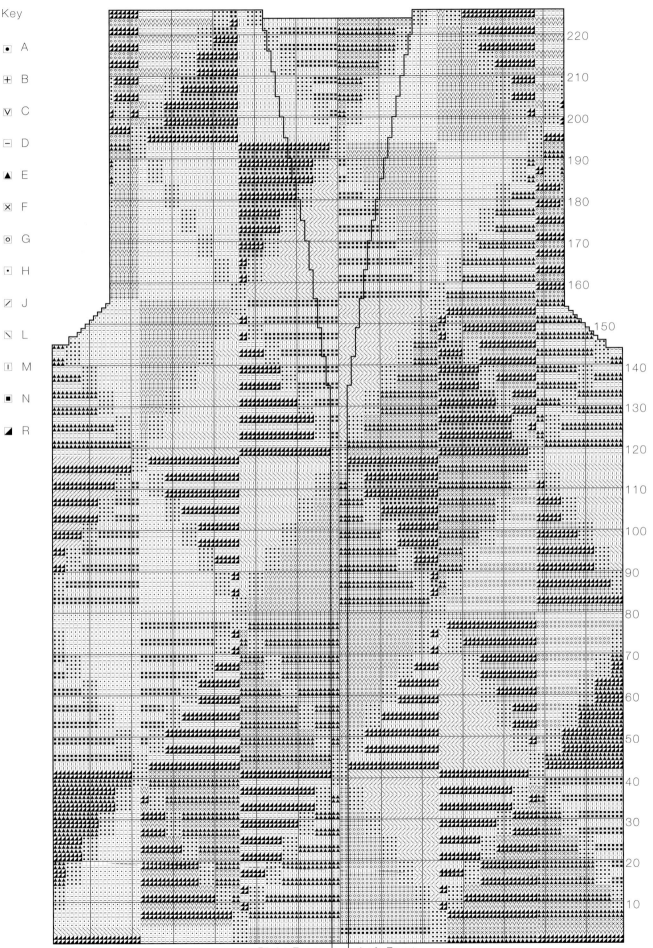

Right Front — — Left Front

43

GYPSY waistcoat

I can never repress the gypsy side of my nature for very long, so accidental colour happenings seduce me every time. Falling across a Guatemalan weaving one day, it intrigued me how the Guatemalans manage to achieve exciting designs from a such a disparate collection of tones, and it is this that I have tried to re-create in this waistcoat. Notice how the electric blue at the pocket and borders gives the other colours a real lift. This kind of pattern knits beautifully as a scarf too (see pages 48–9) and it offers a wonderful way of using up collections of yarns left over from other projects. Just remember to drop in those kick colours now and again.

Yarn

Jaeger Matchmaker Merino DK and Jaeger Matchmaker Merino 4 ply

One size to fit a range of sizes
To fit up to chest   112cm (44 in)

A	Jaeger Matchmaker Merino DK	burgundy (655)	5 x 50g
B	Jaeger Matchmaker Merino DK	petrol blue (872)	3 x 50g
C	Jaeger Matchmaker Merino 4 ply	apple green (713)	2 x 50g*
D	Jaeger Matchmaker Merino 4 ply	heather (701)	2 x 50g*
E	Jaeger Matchmaker Merino 4 ply	dark red (705)	3 x 50g*
F	Jaeger Matchmaker Merino DK	sage green (857)	2 x 50g
G	Jaeger Matchmaker Merino 4 ply	purple-pink (716)	2 x 50g*
H	Jaeger Matchmaker Merino 4 ply	orange (712)	3 x 50g*
J	Jaeger Matchmaker Merino DK	yellow (862)	1 x 50g
L	Jaeger Matchmaker Merino 4 ply	pale pink (694)	1 x 50g*

All yarns marked with an * are to be used double.

Needles

1 pair 3¼mm (no 10/US 3) needles
1 pair 4mm (no 8/US 6) needles
1 3¼mm (no 10/US 3) circular needle
stitch holder

Tension

23 stitches and 30 rows to 10cm (4 in) measured over patterned stocking (stockinette) stitch using 4mm (no 8/US 6) needles.

Pattern tip

When working this pattern weave new colour for next stripe on last 8 stitches of previous stripe, then when starting new stripe weave end of finished stripe across first 8 stitches of row.

BACK

Using 4mm (no 10/US 3) needles, cast on 126 sts with yarn A.
Beg with K row, work 6 rows in st st.
Change to yarn B.
K 3 rows.
Change to yarn A.
Work in st st and stripe sequence as folls and AT THE SAME TIME inc 1 st each end of every 10th row 4 times until 134 sts and 72 rows have been completed.
Work 3 rows in st st with yarn A.
Work 3 rows in st st with yarn F.
Work 3 rows in st st with yarn B.
Work 2 rows in st st with yarn H.
Work 1 row in st st with yarn C.
Work 1 row in st st with yarn H.
Work 1 row in st st with yarn A.
Work 3 rows in st st with yarn D.
Work 3 rows in st st with yarn F.
Work 1 row in st st with yarn A.
Work 1 row in st st with yarn H.
Work 3 rows in st st with yarn A.
Work 3 rows in st st with yarn G.
Work 1 row in st st with yarn B.
Work 3 rows in st st with yarn E.

Work 1 row in st st with yarn C.
Work 1 row in st st with yarn G.
Work 3 rows in st st with yarn C.
Work 1 row in st st with yarn J.
Work 1 row in st st with yarn E.
Work 3 rows in st st with yarn H.
Work 3 rows in st st with yarn L.
Work 1 row in st st with yarn E.
Work 1 row in st st with yarn F.
Work 2 rows in st st with yarn B.
Work 3 rows in st st with yarn A.
Work 1 row in st st with yarn H.
Work 3 rows in st st with yarn A.
Work 2 rows in st st with yarn B.
Work 1 row in st st with yarn J.
Work 1 row in st st with yarn G.
Work 2 rows in st st with yarn D.
Work 3 rows in st st with yarn E.
Work 1 row in st st with yarn A.
Work 1 row in st st with yarn C.
Work 3 rows in st st with yarn F.
Work 1 row in st st with yarn B.
Work 3 rows in st st with yarn H.
Work 1 row in st st with yarn E.
Work 2 rows in st st with yarn B.
Work 1 row in st st with yarn L.

Work 1 row in st st with yarn E.
Work 1 row in st st with yarn D.
Work 3 rows in st st with yarn A.
Work 1 row in st st with yarn J.
Work 5 rows in st st with yarn C.
Work 3 rows in st st with yarn F.
Work 1 row in st st with yarn E.
Work 2 rows in st st with yarn H.
Work 3 rows in st st with yarn L.
Work 2 rows in st st with yarn D.
Work 1 row in st st with yarn A.
Work 1 row in st st with yarn J.
Work 1 row in st st with yarn D.
Work 2 rows in st st with yarn E.
Work 4 rows in st st with yarn H.
Work 3 rows in st st with yarn F.
Work 1 row in st st with yarn J.
Work 1 row in st st with yarn E.
Work 3 rows in st st with yarn A.
Work 1 row in st st with yarn B.
Work 2 rows in st st with yarn G.
Work 1 row in st st with yarn B.
Work 2 rows in st st with yarn A.
Work 1 row in st st with yarn C.
Work 2 rows in st st with yarn F.
Work 2 rows in st st with yarn B.

Work 1 row in st st with yarn E.
Work 4 rows in st st with yarn D.
Work 1 row in st st with yarn H.
Work 2 rows in st st with yarn A.
Work 3 rows in st st with yarn H.
Work 2 rows in st st with yarn C.
Work 3 rows in st st with yarn E.
Rep stripe sequence throughout work.

Shape armholes
Cont in stripe sequence as set, cast off (bind off) 4 sts at beg of next 2 rows. 126 sts.
Dec 1 st each end of next 11 rows. 104 sts.
Cont without shaping in stripe sequence as set until 140 rows have been completed.

Shape back neck
Divide for neck shaping on next row as folls:
Next row: Keeping stripe sequence correct, work in patt until 40 sts on right-hand needle, turn, leaving rem sts on stitch holder.
Work each side of neck separately.
Next row: Cast off (bind off) 5 sts, work in st st to end.
Next row: Cast off (bind off) 10 sts, work in st st to end.
Rep last 2 rows. 10 sts.
Cast off (bind off) rem 10 sts.
With RS facing, rejoin yarn to rem sts, cast off (bind off) centre 24 sts, work in st st to end.
Complete other side to match, reversing shapings.

POCKET LININGS (MAKE TWO)
Using 4mm (no 8/US 6) needles, cast on 32 sts with yarn A.
Beg with a K row, work 34 rows in st st.
Leave all sts on stitch holder.

LEFT FRONT
Using 4mm (no 8/US 6) needles, cast on 1 st with yarn H.
Work in st st and stripe sequence as folls and AT THE SAME TIME inc 1 st each end of next

13 rows then inc 1 st on front edge on every row and 1 st on side edge on every alt (other) row until 57 sts, then work 1 row without shaping, thus ending with a WS row.
Work 2 rows in st st with yarn H.
Work 3 rows in st st with yarn F.
Work 1 row in st st with yarn J.
Work 1 row in st st with yarn E.
Work 3 rows in st st with yarn A.
Work 1 row in st st with yarn B.
Work 1 row in st st with yarn G.
Work 1 row in st st with yarn B.
Work 2 rows in st st with yarn A.
Work 1 row in st st with yarn C.
Work 3 rows in st st with yarn F.
Work 2 rows in st st with yarn B.
Work 1 row in st st with yarn E.
Work 4 rows in st st with yarn D.
Work 1 row in st st with yarn H.
Work 1 row in st st with yarn A.
Work 2 rows in st st with yarn H.
Work 2 rows in st st with yarn C.
Work 2 rows in st st with yarn E.
Cont in st st and stripe sequence as given for Back and AT THE SAME TIME inc 1 st at side edge on every 10th row 4 times and AT THE SAME TIME place pocket after 24 rows of stripe sequence for Back have been completed as folls:

Place pocket
Keeping stripe sequence correct, join in pocket lining on next row as folls:
Next row (RS): Work 12 sts in st st, slip next 32 sts onto stitch holder, in place of these sts work in st st across 32 sts from first pocket lining, work in st st to end.
Keeping stripe sequence correct, cont without shaping until 72 rows have been worked, thus ending with a WS row.

Shape armhole and neck
Next row: Cast off (bind off) 4 sts, work in st st to end. 57 sts.

Dec 1 st at neck edge on next and every foll 5th row 10 times and then every foll 3rd row 5 times and AT THE SAME TIME dec 1 st at armhole edge on next 11 rows. 30 sts.
Cont without shaping until Left Front has same number of rows as Back to shoulder, thus ending with a WS row.

Shape shoulders
Cast off (bind off) 10 sts at beg of next and foll alt (other) row. 10 sts.
Cont without shaping for 1 further row.
Cast off (bind off) rem 10 sts.

RIGHT FRONT
Work as given for Left Front, reversing all shapings and placing of pocket.

FINISHING
Press all pieces on WS with a warm iron over a damp cloth. Join both shoulder seams using backstitch or mattress stitch.
Left Front lower edge
With RS facing, using 3¼mm (no 10/US 3) needles with yarn B, pick up and K 40 sts from opening edge to centre of point, 1 st at centre of point, 40 sts to side edge. 81 sts.
Next row: K to end.
Change to yarn A.
Next row: K39, sl1, k2tog, psso, K to end.
Next row: P to end.
Rep last 2 rows, dec as set, a further 2 times.
Cast off (bind off) loosely and evenly.
Right Front lower band
Work as given for Left Front lower band.
Neck and front bands (worked in one piece)
With RS facing, using 3¼mm (no 10/US 3) circular needle with yarn A, pick up and K 62 sts from bottom of Right Front to beg of neck shaping, 72 sts up Right Front neck, 44 sts across Back neck, 72 sts down Left Front neck, 62 sts down Left Front to bottom

edge. 312 sts.

Beg with a P row, work 5 rows in st st in stripe sequence as folls:

Work 2 rows in st st with yarn A.

Work 1 row in st st with yarn H.

Work 1 row in st st with yarn E.

Work 1 row in st st with yarn D.

Change to yarn B.

K 3 rows.

Change to yarn A.

Beg with a K row, work 6 rows in st st.

Cast off (bind off) loosely and evenly.

Armhole bands

With RS facing, using 3¼mm (no 10/US 3) needles with yarn A, pick up and K 130 sts evenly around armhole edge.

Beg with a P row, work 2 rows in st st.

Next row: P 2 sts with yarn A, * P 2 sts with yarn B, P 2 sts with yarn A, rep from * to end.

Next row: K 2 sts with yarn A, * K 2 sts with yarn B, K 2 sts with yarn A, rep from * to end.

Change to yarn A.

P 3 rows.

Work 5 rows in st st.

Cast off (bind off) loosely and evenly.

Pocket tops

With RS facing, slip 32 sts from stitch holder onto 3¼mm (no 10/US 3) needle.

Beg with a K row, work 2 rows in st st.

Next row: * K 2 sts with yarn A, K 2 sts with yarn, rep from * to end.

Next row: * P 2 sts with yarn A, P 2 sts with yarn B, rep from * to end.

Change to yarn A.

K 3 rows.

Work 5 rows in st st.

Cast off (bind off) loosely and evenly.

Join side seams using mattress stitch. Catch down pocket linings on WS. Fold all border to WS at foldline ridge and sew into place. See the basic information (page 13) for further finishing instructions.

GYPSY scarf

Yarn

Jaeger Matchmaker Merino DK and Jaeger Matchmaker Merino 4 ply

One size to fit a range of sizes

A	Jaeger Matchmaker Merino DK	burgundy (655)	2 x 50g
B	Jaeger Matchmaker Merino DK	petrol blue (872)	1 x 50g
C	Jaeger Matchmaker Merino 4 ply	apple green (713)	1 x 50g*
D	Jaeger Matchmaker Merino 4 ply	heather (701)	1 x 50g*
E	Jaeger Matchmaker Merino 4 ply	dark red (705)	1 x 50g*
F	Jaeger Matchmaker Merino DK	sage green (857)	1 x 50g
G	Jaeger Matchmaker Merino 4 ply	purple-pink (716)	1 x 50g*
H	Jaeger Matchmaker Merino 4 ply	orange (712)	1 x 50g*
J	Jaeger Matchmaker Merino DK	yellow (862)	1 x 50g
L	Jaeger Matchmaker Merino 4 ply	pale pink (694)	1 x 50g*

All yarns marked with an * are to be used double.

Needles

1 pair 4mm (no 8/US 6) needles
crochet hook

Tension

23 stitches and 30 rows to 10cm (4 in) measured over patterned stocking (stockinette) stitch using 4mm (no 8/US 6) needles.

Pattern tip

When working this pattern weave new colour for next stripe on last 8 stitches of previous stripe, then when starting new stripe weave end of finished stripe across first 8 stitches of row.

SCARF

Using 4mm (no 8/US 6) needles, cast on 64 sts with yarn A.
Work in st st and foll stripe sequence as given for Back of Gypsy waistcoat (see page 44) working patt rep 3 times.
Change to yarn A.

Beg with a K row, work 3 rows in st st.
Cast off (bind off) loosely and evenly.

FINISHING

Using a crochet hook with yarn E, work 1 row of double crochet at each short end.
Change to yarn B.

Work 1 further row of double crochet at each short end.
Press on WS with a warm iron over a damp cloth. See the basic information (page 13) for further finishing instructions.

CUT DIAMONDS v-neck sweater

Walking through a local flea market one Sunday morning, I spotted, draped over a shop doorway, an Indian paisley patterned shawl in shades of russett reds and browns, like polished red wood. The shawl sported an expansive border of small diamond motifs on a striped background of soft dusty red, rich amber and deep blue. Based on this layout, I chose 4 ply yarns in shades of deep red, magenta and tangerine to create my background for shaded diamonds of gold silk to give the feel of a tinkling metallic curtain. I've used a fiery palette here though you might be attracted by cooler colours like aqua blue with vibrant green and shades of silver for the diamonds motifs. The garment is finished with a moss stitch (seed stitch) border with a vent up the side to allow for more movement.

Yarn

Jaeger Sienna, Jaeger Pure Cotton, Jaeger Silk, Jaeger Alpaca and Rowan 4 ply Cotton

One size to fit a range of sizes
To fit up to bust   117cm (46 in)

A	Jaeger Sienna	lime green (412)	1 x 50g
B	Jaeger Pure Cotton	natural (532)	1 x 50g
C	Jaeger Silk	gold (134)	3 x 50g
D	Rowan 4 ply Cotton	fuchsia (106)	2 x 50g
E	Jaeger Sienna	dark red (413)	2 x 50g
F	Rowan 4 ply Cotton	red-brown (117)	1 x 50g
G	Rowan 4 ply Cotton	orange (105)	1 x 50g
H	Jaeger Alpaca	red (388)	1 x 50g
I	Rowan 4 ply Cotton	pale purple (104)	1 x 50g
J	Rowan 4 ply Cotton	pink-red (107)	1 x 50g

Needles

1 pair 2¼mm (no 13/US 1) needles
1 pair 3mm (no 11/US 2) needles
stitch holder

Tension

27 stitches and 32 rows to 10cm (4 in) measured over patterned stocking (stockinette) stitch using 3mm (no 11/US 2) needles.

BACK

Using 2¼mm (no 13/US 1) needles, cast on 160 sts with yarn E.
Change to yarn D.
Work 10 rows in moss st (seed st).

Begin chart pattern

Change to 3mm (no 11/US 2) needles.
Using the Fair Isle technique described in the basic information (see page 11), knitting in yarns as required, reading odd numbered K rows from right to left and even numbered P rows from left to right, beg with a K row, work in patt from 60 row patt rep, which is worked entirely in st st, and AT THE SAME TIME keeping moss st (seed st) border as folls:
Next row: Work 10 sts in moss st (seed st) with yarn D, work in patt until 10 sts changing yarns as necessary, work in moss st (seed st) to end with yarn D.
Keeping patt correct, cont as set until chart row 12 has been completed, thus ending with a WS row.
Next row: Work in patt to end, thus incorporating first 10 sts and last 10 sts into patt.
Keeping patt correct, cont without shaping until work measures 71cm (28 in) ending with a WS row.

Shape back neck

Divide for neck shaping on next row as folls:
Next row (RS): Work in patt until 60 sts on right-hand needle, turn, leaving rem sts on stitch holder.
Work each side of neck separately.
Next row: Keeping chart correct, cast off (bind off) 4 sts, work in patt to end. 56 sts.
Cast off (bind off) rem 56 sts.
With RS facing, rejoin yarn to rem sts, cast off (bind off) centre 40 sts, work in patt to end.
Complete to match first side, reversing shapings.

FRONT

Work as given for Back until work measures 46cm, thus ending with a WS row.

Shape neck

Divide for neck shaping on next row as folls:
Next row (RS): Work in patt until 80 sts on right-hand needle, turn, leaving rem sts on stitch holder.
Keeping patt correct, dec 1 st at neck edge on every 3rd row until 56 sts rem.
Cont without shaping until Front has same number of rows as Back to shoulder, thus ending with a WS row.
Cast off (bind off) rem 56 sts.
With RS facing, rejoin yarn to rem sts, work in patt to end.
Complete to match first side, reversing shapings.

SLEEVES (MAKE TWO)

Using 2¼mm (no 13/US 1) needles, cast on 68 sts with yarn E.
Change to yarn D.
Work 10 rows in moss st (seed st).

Begin chart pattern

Change to 3mm (no 11/US 2) needles.
Using the Fair Isle technique described in the basic information (see page 11), knitting in yarns as required, reading odd numbered K rows from right to left and even numbered P rows from left to right, beg with a K row, work in patt from 60 row patt rep sleeve chart, which is worked entirely in st st, taking all inc sts into patt, inc 1 st at each end of 4th and every foll 4th row until 136 sts.
Cont without shaping for 8 further rows.
Cast off (bind off) rem 136 sts.

CUT DIAMONDS v-neck sweater

FINISHING

Press all pieces on WS with a warm iron over
a damp cloth. Join right shoulder seam using
backstitch or mattress stitch.

Neckband

With RS facing, using 2¼mm (no 13/US 1)
needles with yarn D, pick up and K 79 sts
down Left Front neck, 1 st for centre of
v-neck (mark this st), 79 sts up Right Front
neck, and 45 sts across Back neck. 204 sts.

Row 1: Beg with a P st, work 121 sts in
moss st (seed st), K1, P2tog tbl, P1, P2tog,
K1, beg with a P st, work in moss st (seed st)
to end.

Row 2: Beg with a K st, work 75 sts in moss
st (seed st), K1, K2tog tbl, K1, K2tog, K1,
work in moss st (seed st) to end.

Cont in moss st (seed st) working dec as set
on each side of marked stitch for 6 further
rows.

Change to yarn E.

Work 1 row in moss st (seed st).

Cast off (bind off) in moss st (seed st).

Join left shoulder seam. Sew in sleeves using
backstitch or mattress stitch, matching centre
of sleeves to shoulder seam. Join side seams
and sleeve seams using backstitch or
mattress stitch. See the basic information
(page 13) for further finishing instructions.

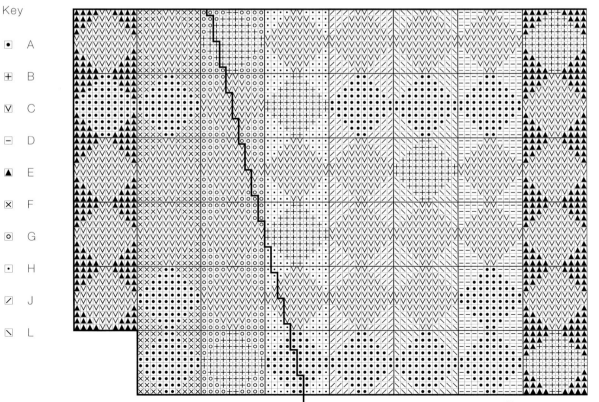

Key

⊡	A
⊞	B
Ⅴ	C
⊟	D
▲	E
⊠	F
⊙	G
⊡	H
⊿	J
⊾	L

Sleeve

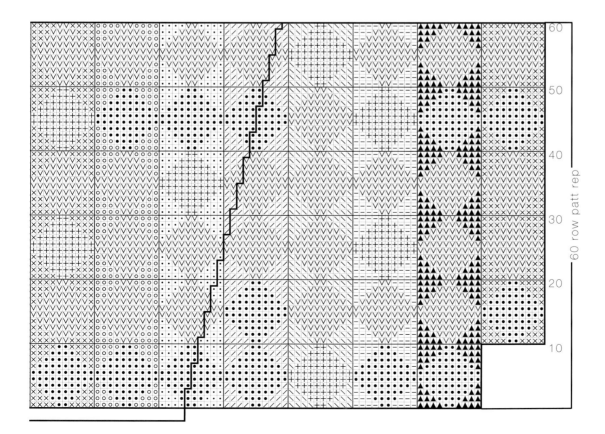

60 row patt rep

OLIVES v-neck cardigan

Don't you just love all the creative breads that now grace our supermarket shelves? The one that I particularly like is bread with sliced olives, and while slicing a loaf one day the oval shapes of the olives leapt out at me as being a perfect design idea. To avoid having flat, predictable circles like doughnuts, I gave the circle shape a little wobble by using two shades of purple, one in chenille the other in cotton. The background is knitted in reverse stocking stitch, while the ovals are in the more traditional stocking stitch. With only three colours needed for the whole design, this design is fabulous to work in your own colourway. Deep reds on a cobalt blue could be a shocker.

Yarn

Rowan Handknit DK Cotton and Rowan Fine Cotton Chenille

One size to fit a range of sizes
To fit up to bust   107cm (42 in)

A	Rowan Handknit DK Cotton	lime green (219)	9 x 50g
B	Rowan Handknit DK Cotton	pale purple (223)	2 x 50g
C	Rowan Fine Cotton Chenille	plum (409)	2 x 50g

Needles

1 pair 3¼mm (no 10/US 3) needles
1 pair 4mm (no 8/US 6) needles
1 3¼mm (no 10/US 3) circular needle
stitch holder

Buttons

5

Tension

20 stitches and 28 rows to 10cm (4 in) measured over patterned stocking (stockinette) stitch using 4mm (no 8/US 6) needles.

BACK

Using 3¼mm (no 10/US 3) needles, cast on 106 sts with yarn A.

Work hem

Beg with a K row, work 9 rows in st st, thus ending with a WS row.
Change to yarn B.
P 3 rows to form hemline ridge, thus ending with a RS row.
Change to yarn A,
Beg with a K row, work a further 5 rows in st st, thus ending with a WS row.

Begin chart pattern

Change to 4mm (no 8/US 6) needles.
Using the intarsia technique described in the basic information (see page 10), joining in and breaking off colours as required, reading odd numbered RS rows from right to left and even numbered WS rows from left to right, beg with a RS row, work in patt from body chart, which is worked mainly in reverse st st until, chart row 74 has been completed, thus ending with a WS row.

Shape armholes

Keeping chart correct, cast off (bind off) 8 sts at beg of next 2 rows. 90 sts.
Cont without shaping until chart row 148 has been completed, thus ending with a WS row.

Shape shoulders and back neck

Keeping chart correct, cast off (bind off) 10 sts at beg of next 2 rows. 70 sts.
Divide for neck shaping on next row as folls:
Next row (RS): Cast off (bind off) 9 sts, work in patt until 15 st on right-hand needle, turn, leaving rem sts on stitch holder.
Work each side of neck separately.
Next row: Cast off (bind off) 5 sts, patt to end.
Cast off (bind off) rem 10 sts.
With RS facing, rejoin yarn to rem sts on stitch holder, slip centre 22 sts on stitch holder for neckband, work in patt to end.
Complete to match first side, reversing shapings.

LEFT FRONT

Using 3¼mm (no 10/US 3) needles, cast on 50 sts with yarn A.

Work hem

Beg with a K row, work 9 rows in st st, thus ending with a WS row.
Change to yarn B.
P 3 rows to form hemline ridge, thus ending with a RS row.
Change to yarn A.
Beg with a K row, work a further 5 rows in st st, thus ending with a WS row.

Begin chart pattern

Change to 4mm (no 8/US 6) needles.
Using the intarsia technique described in the basic information (see page 10), joining in and breaking off colours as required, reading odd numbered RS rows from right to left and even numbered WS rows from left to right, beg with a RS row, work in patt from left front chart, which is worked mainly in reverse st st, until chart row 74 has been completed, thus ending with a WS row.

Shape armhole

Next row (RS): Cast off (bind off) 8 sts, work in patt to end. 42 sts.
Cont without shaping until chart row 79 has been completed, thus ending with a RS row at neck edge.

Shape front neck

Dec 1 st at neck edge on next and every foll 6th row until 31 sts rem.
Dec 1 st at front edge of every foll 4th row until 29 sts rem.
Cont without shaping until Front has same number of rows as Back to shoulder, thus ending with a WS row.

Shape shoulder

Next row: Cast off (bind off) 10 sts, patt to end. 19 sts.
Cont without shaping for 1 further row.
Next row: Cast off (bind off) 9 sts, patt to end. 10 sts.
Cont without shaping for 1 further row.
Cast off (bind off) rem 10 sts.

RIGHT FRONT

Work as given for Left Front but foll chart for Right Front, reversing all shapings.

SLEEVES (MAKE TWO)

Using 3¼mm (no 10/US 3) needles, cast on 48 sts with yarn A.
Beg with a K row, work 9 rows in st st, thus ending with a WS row.
Change to yarn B.
P 3 rows to form hemline ridge, thus ending

with a RS row.

Change to yarn A.

Beg with a K row, work 5 rows in st st, thus ending with a WS row.

Begin chart pattern

Change to 4mm (no 8/US 6) needles.

Using the intarsia technique described in the basic information (see page 10), joining in and breaking off colours as required, reading odd numbered RS rows from right to left and even numbered WS rows from left to right, beg with a RS row, work in patt from sleeve chart, which is worked mainly in reverse st st, until chart row 10 has been completed, thus ending with a WS row.

Keeping chart correct, taking all inc sts into patt, inc 1 st at each end of next and every foll 6th row until 62 sts and then inc 1 st at each end of every foll 4th row until 106 sts.

Cont without shaping until chart row 142 has been completed, thus ending with a WS row.

Cast off (bind off) loosely and evenly.

FINISHING

Press all pieces on WS with a warm iron over a damp cloth. Join both shoulder seams using backstitch or mattress stitch. Join side seams using backstitch or mattress stitch. Fold bottom hem onto WS along hemline ridge and slip-stitch into position.

Neck and front band (knitted in one piece)

With RS facing, using 3¼mm (no 10/US 3) circular needle with yarn A, pick up and K 55

sts up Right Front to beg of neck shaping, 48 sts up Right Front neck, 30 sts across Back neck, 48 sts down Left Front neck, and 55 sts down Left Front. 236 sts.

Beg with a P row, work 3 rows in st st.

Make buttonholes

1st buttonhole row: K3, * cast off (bind off) 2 sts knitwise, K until 10 sts on right-hand needle after last cast-off (bind-off), rep from * 3 times, cast off (bind off) 2 sts, K to end.

2nd buttonhole row: P across all sts casting on 2 sts over those cast off (bound off) on previous row.

Next row: K to end.

Change to yarn B.

P 3 rows.

Change to yarn A.

Work 2 rows in st st.

Work 1st and 2nd buttonhole rows again.

Work 1 row.

Cast off (bind off).

Sew in sleeves using mattress stitch, matching centre of sleeves to shoulder seam. Fold all hems onto WS along hemline ridge and slip-stitch into position. Oversew double buttonholes. Sew buttons on to correspond with buttonholes. See the basic information (page 13) for further finishing instructions.

OLIVES v-neck cardigan

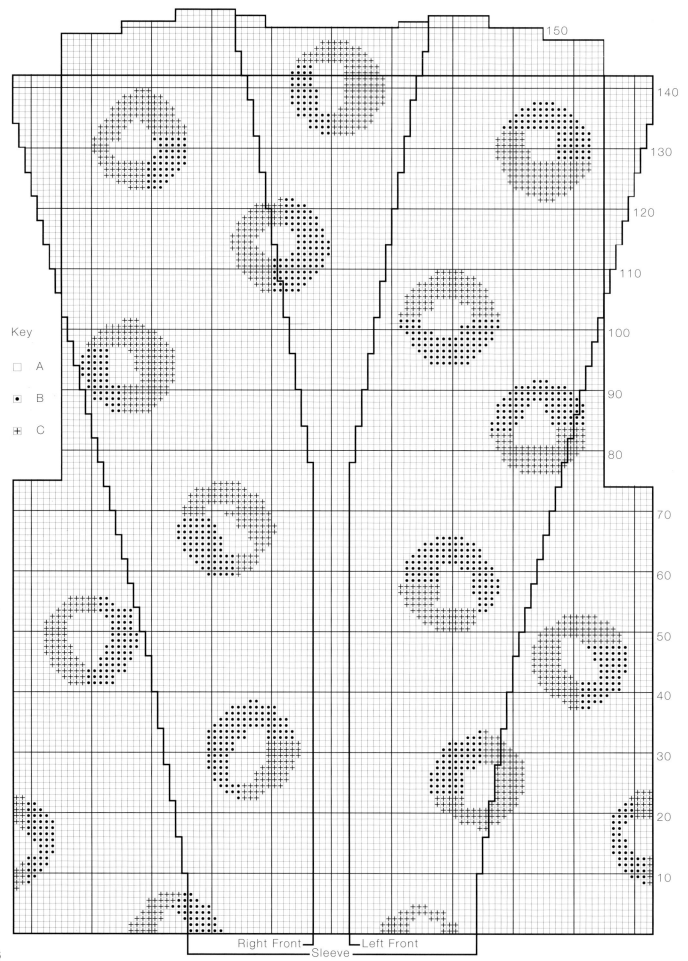

Key

☐ A

⊡ B

✛ C

150

140

130

120

110

100

90

80

70

60

50

40

30

20

10

Right Front — Left Front

— Sleeve —

OLD TILES box jacket

Some of you may recognise this garment I designed for the Rowan collection. It has proved popular with all age groups. Knitted in Rowan Cotton Glacé, Rowan Fine Cotton Chenille and Rowan Kid Silk it is quite luxurious yet lightweight to wear. I'm crazy about deteriorating surfaces and half demolished derelict buildings – beautiful tiled surfaces found in of historical houses and places of disrepute are often left with half told stories in their deteriorating state. The design inspiration came from a photograph of a weathered and corroding town wall in Portugal – the type of surface I get such a thrill from because of its sense of mystery. The several shades of lemon and acid yellow give this whole palette a sharpness and the rust brown, a warmth. If any of the colours in this garment are not in your local yarn shop, don't stop there – substitute and play around with the colours.

Yarn

Rowan Cotton Glacé, Rowan Fine Cotton Chenille and Rowan Kid Silk

One size to fit a range of sizes
To fit up to bust   112cm (44 in)

A	Rowan Cotton Glacé	dusky brown (439)	6 x 50g
B	Rowan Cotton Glacé	pale blue (749)	1 x 50g
C	Rowan Cotton Glacé	green-yellow (780)	1 x 50g
D	Rowan Cotton Glacé	salmon pink (783)	1 x 50g
E	Rowan Cotton Glacé	pale beige (730)	1 x 50g
F	Rowan Cotton Glacé	butter yellow (795)	1 x 50g
G	Rowan Cotton Glacé	pale pink (747)	1 x 50g
H	Rowan Fine Cotton Chenille	lime green (411)	1 x 50g
J	Rowan Kid Silk	opal (976)	1 x 50g
L	Rowan Kid Silk	yellow (973)	1 x 50g
M	Rowan Kid Silk	gold (989)	1 x 50g
N	Rowan Kid Silk	mid beige (997)	2 x 50g
Q	Rowan Kid Silk	raspberry pink (968)	2 x 50g
R	Rowan Kid Silk	orange (971)	2 x 50g
S	Rowan Kid Silk	brown-gold (972)	1 x 50g
T	Rowan Kid Silk	green (970)	1 x 50g
U	Rowan Kid Silk	dark dusky rose (996)	1 x 50g

Needles

1 pair 2¾mm (no 12/US 2) needles
1 pair 3¼mm (no 10/US 3) needles
stitch holder

Buttons

7

Tension

23 stitches and 32 rows to 10cm (4 in) measured over patterned stocking (stockinette) stitch using 3¼mm (no 10/US 3) needles.

BACK

Using 2¾mm (no 12/US 2) needles, cast on 128 sts with yarn A.

Work hem

Beg with a K row, work 9 rows in st st, thus ending with a RS row.

Next row (WS): K to end to form hemline ridge.

Begin chart pattern

Change to 3¼mm (no 10/US 3) needles. Using the intarsia technique described in the basic information (see page 10), joining in and breaking off colours as required, reading odd numbered K rows from right to left and even numbered P rows from left to right, beg with a K row, work in patt from body chart, which is worked entirely in st st, until chart row 86 has been completed, thus ending with a WS row.

Shape armholes

Keeping chart correct, cast off (bind off) 6 sts at beg next 2 rows. 116 sts.
Cont without shaping until chart row 158 has been completed, thus ending with a WS row.

Shape shoulders and back neck

Keeping chart correct, cast off (bind off) 13 sts at beg next 2 rows. 90 sts.
Divide for neck shaping on next row as folls:
Next row (RS): Cast off (bind off) 14 sts, work in patt until 18 sts on right-hand needle, turn, leaving rem sts on stitch holder.
Work each side of neck separately.
Next row: Cast off (bind off) 4 sts, work in patt to end.
Cast off (bind off) rem 14 sts.
With RS facing, rejoin yarns to rem sts on stitch holder, cast off (bind off) 26 sts for centre back neck, work in patt to end. 32 sts.
Complete to match first side, reversing all shapings.

POCKET LININGS (MAKE TWO)

Using 3¼mm (no 10/US 3) needles, cast on 30 sts with yarn A.
Beg with a K row, work 40 rows in st st, thus ending with a WS row.
Leave all sts on stitch holder.

LEFT FRONT

Using 2¾mm (no 12/US 2) needles, cast on 64 sts with yarn A.

Work hem

Beg with a K row, work 9 rows in st st, thus ending with a RS row.

Next row (WS): K to end to form hemline ridge.

Begin chart pattern

Change to 3¼mm (no 10/US 3) needles. Using the intarsia technique described in the basic information (see page 10), joining in and breaking off colours as required, reading

odd numbered K rows from right to left and even numbered P rows from left to right, beg with a K row, work in patt from left front chart, which is worked entirely in st st, until chart row 48 has been completed, thus ending with a WS row.

Place pocket

Keeping chart correct, join in pocket lining on next row as folls:

Next row (RS): Work 20 sts in patt, slip next 30 sts onto stitch holder, in place of these sts work in patt across 30 sts from first pocket lining, work in patt to end.

Cont without shaping until chart row 86 has been worked, thus ending with a WS row.

Shape armhole

Next row (RS): Cast off (bind off) 6 sts, work in patt to end. 58 sts.

Cont without shaping until chart row 137 has been worked, thus ending with a RS row.

Shape front neck

Next row (WS): Cast off (bind off) 6 sts, work in patt to end. 52 sts.

Cont without shaping for 1 further row.

Next row (WS): Cast off (bind off) 3 sts, work in patt to end. 49 sts.

Dec 1 st at neck edge on next 6 rows and then on every alt (other) row 2 further times. 41 sts.

Cont without shaping until Front has same number of rows as Back to shoulder, thus ending with a WS row.

Shape shoulder

Next row (RS): Cast off (bind off) 13 sts, work in patt to end. 28 sts.

Cont without shaping for 1 further row.

Next row (RS): Cast off (bind off) 14 sts, work in patt to end. 14 sts.

Cont without shaping for 1 further row.

Cast off (bind off) rem 14 sts.

RIGHT FRONT

Work as given for Left Front but foll right front chart, reversing all shapings and placing of pocket.

SLEEVES (MAKE TWO)

Using 2³/₄mm (no 12/US 2) needles, cast on 52 sts with yarn A.

Work hem

Beg with a K row, work 9 rows in st st, thus ending with a RS row.

Next row (WS): K to end to form hemline ridge.

Begin chart pattern

Change to 3³/₄mm (no 10/US 3) needles. Using the intarsia technique described in the basic information (see page 10), joining in and breaking off colours as required, reading odd numbered K rows from right to left and even numbered P rows from left to right, beg with a K row, work in patt from sleeve chart, which is worked entirely in st st, and AT THE SAME TIME inc 1 st at each end on 11th row and every foll 6th row until 84 sts then on every foll 4th row until 104 sts.

Keeping chart correct, cont without shaping until chart row 154 has been worked, thus ending with a WS row.

Cast off (bind off) loosely and evenly.

FINISHING

Press all pieces on WS with a warm iron over a damp cloth. Join both shoulder seams using backstitch or mattress stitch.

Buttonhole band

With RS of Right Front facing, using 2³/₄mm (no 12/US 2) needles with yarn A, pick up and K 102 sts up opening edge from hemline ridge to beg of neck shaping.

Next row (WS): P to end.

1st buttonhole row: K2, (cast off (bind off) 2 sts knitwise, K until 14 sts on right-hand needle after last cast off (bind off)) 6 times, cast off (bind off) 2 sts knitwise, K to end.

2nd buttonhole row: P across row casting on 2 sts over those cast off (bound off) on previous row.

Next row (RS): P to end to form hemline ridge.

3rd buttonhole row: P2, [cast off (bind off) 2 sts purlwise, P until 14 sts on right-hand needle after last cast off (bind off)] 6 times, cast off (bind off) 2 sts purlwise, P to end.

4th button hole row: K across row casting on 2 sts over those cast off (bound off) on previous row.

Work 3 rows in st st.

Cast off (bind off) loosely and evenly.

Button band

Work as given for buttonhole band but picking up sts along Left Front and omitting buttonholes.

Neckband

With RS facing, using 2³/₄mm (no 12/US 2) needles with yarn A, pick up and K 34 sts up Right Front neck from hemline ridge at centre front to shoulder, K 34 sts across Back neck and K 34 sts down Left Front neck to hemline ridge at centre front. 102 sts.

Beg with a P row, work 3 rows in st st, thus ending with a WS row.

Next row (RS): P to end to form hemline ridge.

Beg with a P row, work 5 rows in st st.

Cast off (bind off) loosely and evenly.

Pocket tops (both alike)

With RS facing, using 2³/₄mm (no 12/US 2) needles, slip sts from stitch holder onto left-hand needle.

With yarn A and beg with a K row, work 3 rows in st st, thus ending with a RS row.

Next row (WS): K to end to form hemline ridge.

Beg with a K row, work 5 rows in st st.

Cast off (bind off) loosely and evenly.

Sew in sleeves using backstitch or mattress stitch, matching centre of sleeves to shoulder seam. Join side and sleeve seams using backstitch or mattress stitch. Join front band seams. Fold all hems onto WS along hemline ridge and slip-stitch into position. Slip-stitch pocket edging and linings in place. Press seams. Sew on buttons to correspond to buttonholes. See the basic information (page 13) for further finishing instructions.

Key

- ■ A
- ▫ B
- ☒ C
- ◉ D
- ◻ E
- ▼ F
- ⊟ G
- ⊿ H
- ⊞ J
- ⊟ L
- ⊡ M
- ▽ N
- ◥ Q
- ◪ R
- ◢ S
- ▣ T
- ⊍ U

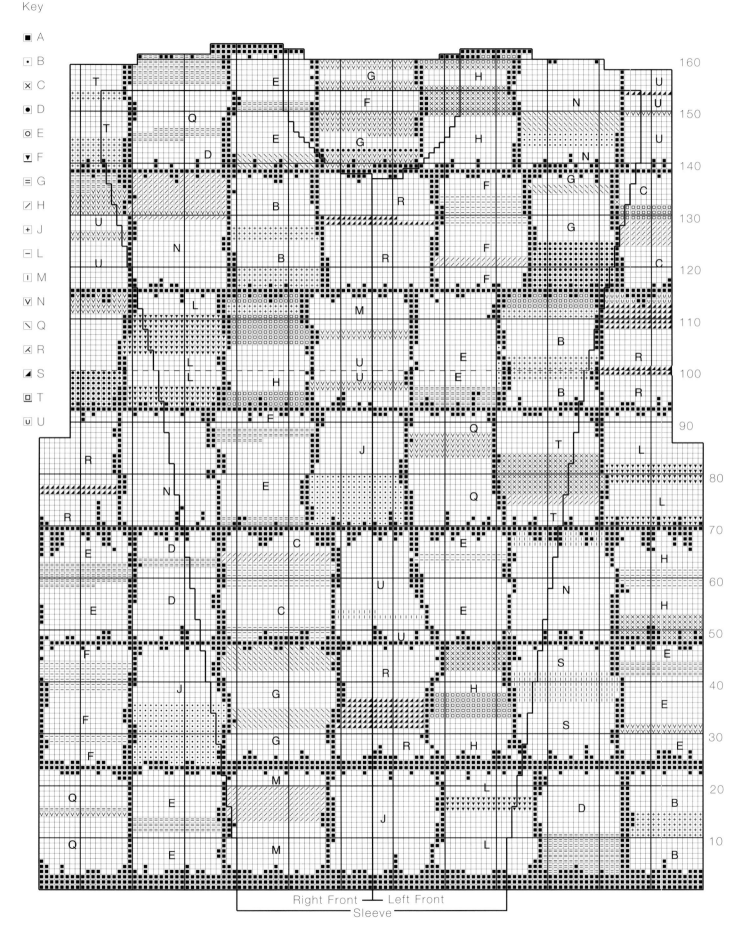

Right Front — Left Front

Sleeve

JOCKEY crewneck sweater

Straight away the name of this garment tells you where the layout for this design came from – horseracing jockeys' uniforms, although I could just as easily have been inspired by quarry tiles and flagstones found in lumber centres or even the street pavement. The idea for splitting the colour for the arms came from the uniforms of the ground staff at airports who guide airplanes into dock. To give this soft pale palette a lift, I have dropped touches of yellow into the expansive cream areas and warm grey and terracotta into the baked clay colour.

Yarn
Rowan DK Tweed and Rowan Felted Tweed

			Extra-small	Small	Medium	Large	Extra-large
To fit up to chest			86.5cm (34 in)	91.5cm (36 in)	96.5cm (38 in)	102cm (40 in)	107cm (42 in)
A	Rowan DK Tweed	rust (864)	4	4	5	5	6 x 50g
B	Rowan Felted Tweed	dark grey (852)	4	4	5	5	5 x 50g
C	Rowan Felted Tweed	purple-pink (139)	1	1	1	1	1 x 50g
D	Rowan Felted Tweed	rose pink (137)	1	1	1	1	2 x 50g
E	Rowan DK Tweed	mustard (863)	4	4	4	5	5 x 50g
F	Rowan DK Tweed	oatmeal (850)	2	2	3	3	3 x 50g
G	Rowan Felted Tweed	gold (136)	1	1	1	1	1 x 50g
H	Rowan DK Tweed	grey-green (851)	1	1	1	1	1 x 50g

Needles
1 pair 3³/₄mm (no 9/US 5) needles
1 pair 4mm (no 8/US 6) needles
stitch holder

Tension
22 stitches and 30 rows to 10cm (4 in) measured over striped stocking (stockinette) stitch using 4mm (no 8/US 6) needles.

FRONT
Using 3³/₄mm (no 9/US 5) needles, cast on 64 (68; 72; 76; 80) sts with yarn E and then 64 (68; 72; 76; 80) sts with yarn A. 128 (136; 144; 152; 160) sts.

Work rib
Using the intarsia technique described in the basic information (see page 10), joining in and breaking off colours as required, work as folls:

Row 1 (RS): Using yarn A K1, P2, (K2, P2) 15 (16; 17; 18; 19) times, K1, using yarn E K1, (P2, K2) 15 (16; 17; 18; 19) times, P2, K1.

Row 2: Using yarn E P1, K2, (P2, K2) 15 (16; 17; 18; 19) times, P1, using yarn A P1, (K2, P2) 15 (16; 17; 18; 19) times, K2, P1.
Rep last 2 rows 14 further times.

Begin chart pattern
Change to 4mm (no 8/US 6) needles.
Using the intarsia technique described in the basic information (see page 10), joining in and breaking off colours as required, reading odd numbered K rows from right to left and even numbered P rows from left to right, beg with a K row, work in stripe sequence from body chart, which is worked entirely in st st, as folls:

Row 1 (RS): K 64 (68; 72; 76; 80) sts using yarn indicated by first 15 sts of row 1 of chart, K rem 64 (68; 72; 76; 80) sts using yarn indicated by last 15 sts of row 1 of chart.
This row sets position of stripe sequence shown on chart.
** Cont in patt from chart until work measures 38 (38; 39; 41; 44) cm, thus ending with a WS row.

Shape armholes
Keeping chart correct, cast off (bind off) 3 sts at beg of next 2 rows. 122 (130; 138; 146; 154) sts.
Dec 1 st at each end of next and foll 2 alt (other) rows. 116 (124; 132; 140; 148 sts.) **
Cont wihtout shaping until armholes measure 19 (20; 20; 21; 21) cm, thus ending with a WS row.

Shape neck
Divide for neck shaping on next row as folls:
Next row (RS): Patt 50 (53; 57; 60; 64) sts, turn, leaving rem sts on stitch holder.
Work each side of neck separately.

Keeping chart correct, cast off (bind off) 4 sts at beg of next row. 46 (49; 53; 56; 60) sts.
Dec 1 st at neck edge on next 7 rows, then on foll 4 alt (other) rows. 35 (38; 42; 45; 49) sts.
Work 1 row, thus ending with a WS row.

Shape shoulder
Cast off (bind off) 12 (13; 14; 15; 16) sts at beg of next and foll alt (other) row.
Work 1 row.
Cast off (bind off) rem 11 (12; 14; 15; 17) sts.
With RS facing, rejoin yarn to rem sts on stitch holder, cast off (bind off) centre 16 (18; 18; 20; 20) sts, work in patt to end.
Complete to match first side, reversing shapings.

BACK
Using 3³/₄mm (no 9/US 5) needles, cast on 64 (68; 72; 76; 80) sts with yarn A, and then 64 (68; 72; 76; 80) sts with yarn E, thus reversing positioning of colour blocks for Back. 128 (136; 144; 152; 160) sts.

Work rib
Using the intarsia technique described in the basic information (see page 10), joining in

and breaking off colours as required, work as folls:

Row 1 (RS): Using yarn E K1, P2, (K2, P2) 15 (16: 17: 18: 19) times, K1, using yarn A K1, (P2, K2) 15 (16: 17: 18: 19) times, P2, K1.

Row 2: Using yarn A P1, K2, (P2, K2) 15 (16: 17: 18: 19) times, P1, using yarn E P1, (K2, P2) 15 (16: 17: 18: 19) times, K2, P1.
Rep last 2 rows 14 further times.

Begin chart pattern

Change to 4mm (no 8/US 6) needles.
Using the intarsia technique described in the basic information (see page 10), joining in and breaking off colours as required, reading odd numbered K rows from right to left and even numbered P rows from left to right, beg with a K row, work in stripe sequence from body chart, which is worked entirely in st st, as folls:

Row 1 (RS): K first 64 (68: 72: 76: 80) sts using yarn indicated by last 15 sts of row 1 of chart, K rem 64 (68: 72: 76: 80) sts using yarn indicated by first 15 sts of row 1 of chart. This row sets position of stripe sequence as shown on chart.
Now work as given for Front from ** to **.
Cont without shaping until Back has same number of rows as Front to start of shoulder shaping, thus ending with a WS row.

Shape shoulders and back neck

Keeping chart correct, cast off (bind off) 12 (13: 14: 15: 16) sts at beg of next 2 rows. (92: 98: 104: 110: 116 sts.)
Divide for neck shaping on next row as folls:

Next row (RS): Cast off (bind off) 12 (13: 14: 15: 16) sts, work in patt until 15 (16: 18: 19: 21) sts on right-hand needle, turn, leaving rem sts on stitch holder.
Work each side of neck separately.
Cast off (bind off) 4 sts at beg of next row.
Cast off (bind off) rem 11 (12: 14: 15: 17) sts.
With RS facing, rejoin yarn to rem sts, cast off (bind off) centre 38 (40: 40: 42: 42) sts, work in patt to end.
Complete to match first side, reversing shapings.

LEFT SLEEVE

Using 3¾mm (no 9/US 5) needles, cast on 58 (58: 62: 62: 66) sts with yarn B.

Work rib

Row 1 (RS): K2, *P2, K2, rep from * to end.
Row 2: P2, *K2, P2, rep from * to end.
Rep last 2 rows 14 further times.

Begin chart pattern

Change to 4mm (no 8/US 6) needles.

Work in st st and foll stripe sequence as shown on left sleeve chart rep 60 rows as required and AT THE SAME TIME inc 1 st at each end of 3rd and every foll alt (other) row until 78 (80: 70: 74: 70) sts, then on every foll 4th row until 110 (114: 114: 118: 118) sts. Cont without shaping until sleeve measures 43 (45: 47: 48: 49) cm or 17 (17¾: 18½: 18¾: 19¼) in, thus ending with a WS row.

Shape top

Keeping chart correct, cast off (bind off) 3 sts at beg of next 2 rows. 104 (108: 108: 112: 112) sts.
Dec 1 st at each end of next and foll 3 alt (other) rows.
Cont without shaping for 1 further row, thus ending with a WS row.
Cast off (bind off) rem 96 (100: 100: 104: 104) sts.

RIGHT SLEEVE

Work as given for Left Sleeve but using yarn A for first 30 rows and then working in 44 row stripe sequence as shown on right sleeve chart.

FINISHING

Press all pieces on WS with a warm iron over a damp cloth. Join right shoulder seam using backstitch or mattress stitch.

Neckband

With RS facing, using 3¾mm (no 9/US 5) needles with yarn B, pick up and K 24 sts down Left Front neck, 16 (18: 18: 20: 20) sts across Front neck, 24 sts up Right Front neck and 46 (48: 48: 50: 50) sts across Back neck. 110 (114: 114: 118: 118) sts.
Work 14 rows in rib as given for sleeves.
Cast off (bind off) loosely and evenly in rib.
Join left shoulder seam. Sew in sleeves using backstitch or mattress stitch, matching centre of sleeves to shoulder seam. Join side and sleeve seams using backstitch or mattress stitch. See the basic information (page 13) for further finishing instructions.

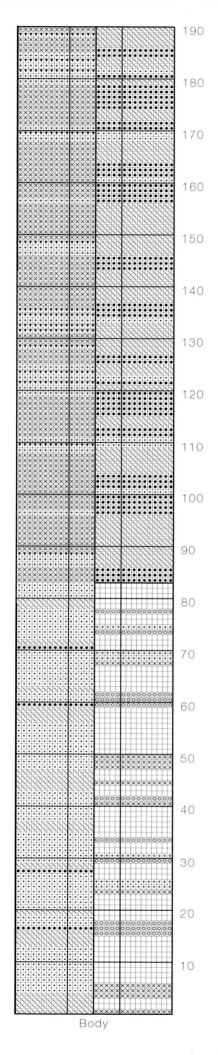

Body

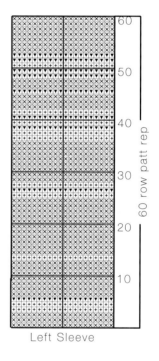

Key

☐ A

☒ B

◉ C

⊞ D

⊡ E

◩ F

● G

▼ H

Left Sleeve

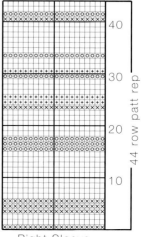

Right Sleeve

65

CHAMPAGNE PLEASE v-neck cardigan

During the long days of winter, I dream of hazy summer days in the countryside with the exquisite filtered light of late afternoons. I think of lovely outdoor summer celebrations, garden parties, flower festivals and wedding receptions where I stand sipping champagne. These elements poured into my imagination when playing with the colours in this garment. Knitted in Rowan Cotton Glacé, I have chosen a misty, sugar-icing blue with dusty lavender and warm cream to work with the dried grass colour of the lattice background. The colours keep the garment looking deliciously light and cool. I particularly enjoy the way this garment works against the pealing paint of this distressed door at an old fisherman's shed with its hints of fawn, blues and sage.

Yarn
Rowan Cotton Glacé

			Extra-small	Small	Medium	Large	Extra-large
	To fit up to bust		81cm (32 in)	86cm (34 in)	91cm (36 in)	97cm (38 in)	102cm (40 in)
A	Rowan Cotton Glacé	green-yellow (780)	7	8	8	8	9 x 50g
B	Rowan Cotton Glacé	pale grey (798)	3	3	3	3	3 x 50g
C	Rowan Cotton Glacé	pale beige (730)	2	2	2	2	2 x 50g
D	Rowan Cotton Glacé	lavender (723)	2	2	2	2	3 x 50g
E	Rowan Cotton Glacé	pale mint green (722)	2	2	2	3	3 x 50g

Needles
1 pair 2³/₄mm (no 12/US 2) needles
1 pair 3¹/₄mm (no 10/US 3) needles
stitch holder

Buttons
5

Tension
23 stitches and 32 rows to 10cm (4 in) measured over patterned stocking (stockinette) stitch using 3¹/₄mm (no 10/US 3) needles.

BACK
Using 2³/₄mm (no 12/US 2) needles, cast on 105 (111; 117; 123; 129) sts with yarn A.

Work hem
Work 8 rows in moss st (seed st).

Begin chart pattern
Change to 3¹/₄mm (no 10/US 3) needles. Using the intarsia technique described in the basic information (see page 10), joining in and breaking off yarns as required, reading odd numbered K rows from right to left and even numbered P rows from left to right, beg with a K row, work in patt from body chart, which is worked entirely in st st, until chart row 8 (10; 10; 12; 12) has been completed, thus ending with a WS row.
Keeping chart correct, dec 1 st at each of next and every foll 4th row until 87 (93; 99; 105; 111) sts rem.
Cont without shaping for 11 further rows.
Keeping chart correct, taking all in sts into patt, inc 1 st at each end of next row and every foll 6th row until 99 (105; 111; 117; 123) sts, then on every foll 4th row until 105 (111; 117; 123; 129) sts.
Cont without shaping for 13 further rows, thus ending with chart row 108 (110; 110; 112; 112).

Shape armholes
Keeping chart correct, cast off (bind off) 4 (4; 5; 5; 6) sts at beg of next 2 rows. 97 (103; 107; 113; 117) sts.
Dec 1 st at each end of next 5 (7; 7; 9; 9) rows, then on every foll alt (other) row until 73 (75; 77; 79; 81) sts rem.
Cont without shaping until chart row 172 (174; 178; 180; 182) has been completed, thus ending with a WS row.

Shape shoulders and back neck
Keeping chart correct, cast off (bind off) 6 (6; 7; 7; 7) sts at beg of next 2 rows. 61 (63; 63; 65; 67) sts.
Divide for neck on next row as folls:

Next row (RS): Cast off (bind off) 6 (6; 7; 7; 7) sts, work in patt until 10 (11; 10; 11; 12) sts on right-hand needle, turn, leaving rem sts on stitch holder.
Work each side of neck separately.

Next row: Cast off (bind off) 4 sts, work in patt to end.
Cast off (bind off) rem 6 (7; 6; 7; 8) sts.
With RS facing, rejoin yarn to rem sts, cast off (bind off) centre 29 sts, work in patt to end.
Complete to match first side, reversing shapings.

LEFT FRONT
Using 2³/₄mm (no 12/US 2) needles, cast on 57 (59; 63; 65; 69) sts with yarn A.

Work hem
Work 7 rows in moss st (seed st) as given for Back.

Next row (WS): Work 5 sts in moss st (seed st), slip these 5 sts onto stitch holder for button border, M1, work in moss st (seed st) to last 0 (1; 0; 1; 0) st, (inc in last st) 0 (1; 0; 1; 0) times. 53 (56; 59; 62; 65) sts.

Begin chart pattern
Change to 3¹/₄mm (no 10/US 3) needles. Using the intarsia technique described in the basic information (see page 10), joining in and breaking off yarns as required, reading odd numbered K rows from right to left and even numbered P rows from left to right, beg with a K row, work in patt from left front chart, which is worked entirely in st st, until chart row 8 (10; 10; 12; 12) has been completed, thus ending with a WS row.
Keeping chart correct, dec 1 st at beg of next and every foll 4th row until 44 (47; 50; 53; 56) sts rem.
Cont without shaping for 11 further rows.
Keeping chart correct, taking all inc sts into

patt, inc 1 st at beg of next and every foll 6th row until 50 (53; 56; 59; 62) sts, then on every foll 4th row until 53 (56; 59; 62; 65) sts. Cont without shaping for 13 further rows, thus ending with chart row 108 (110; 110; 112; 112).

Shape armhole
Keeping chart correct, cast off (bind off) 4 (4; 5; 5; 6) sts at beg of next row. 49 (52; 54; 57; 59) sts.

Cont without shaping for 1 further row.

Dec 1 st at armhole edge on next 5 (4; 4; 2; 2) rows. 44 (48; 50; 55; 57) sts.

Cont without shaping for 1 (0; 0; 0; 0) further row, thus ending with chart row 116.

2nd, 3rd, 4th and 5th sizes only
Keeping chart correct, dec 1 st at armhole edge on next (2; 2; 6; 6) rows and AT THE SAME TIME dec 1 st at front edge on next and foll (0; 0; 2; 2) alt (other) rows. (45; 47; 46; 48) sts.

All sizes
Keeping chart correct, dec 1 st at each end of next and foll 6 (7; 8; 8; 8) alt (other) rows. 30 (29; 29; 28; 30) sts.

5th size only
Cont without shaping for 1 further row.
Dec 1 st at armhole edge on next row.
29 sts.

All sizes
Cont without shaping for 1 further row.
Dec 1 st at front slope edge only on next and foll 4 (2; 1; 0; 0) alt rows, then on every foll 4th row until 18 (19; 20; 21; 22) sts rem. Cont without shaping until chart row 172 (174; 178; 180; 182) has been completed, ending with a WS row.

Shape shoulder
Cast off (bind off) 6 (6; 7; 7; 7) sts at beg of next and foll alt (other) row.
Cont without shaping for 1 further row.
Cast off (bind off) rem 6 (7; 6; 7; 8) sts.

RIGHT FRONT
Using 2³/₄mm (no 12/US 2) needles, cast on 57 (59; 63; 65; 69) sts with yarn.

Work hem
Work 4 rows in moss st (seed st) as given for Back.

Next row (buttonhole row): Work 2 sts in moss st (seed st), yrn (to make a buttonhole), work 2 tog, work in moss st (seed st) to end. Work 2 further rows in moss st (seed st).

Next row (WS): (Inc in first st) 0 (1; 0; 1; 0) times, work in moss st (seed st) to last 5 sts, M1, turn, leaving last 5 sts on stitch holder for

buttonhole border. 53 (56; 59; 62; 65) sts.

Begin chart pattern
Change to 3¹/₄mm (no 10/US 3) needles. Using the intarsia technique described in the basic information (see page 10), joining in and breaking off yarns as required, reading odd numbered K rows from right to left and even numbered P rows from left to right, beg with a K row, work in patt from right front chart, which is worked entirely in st st, until chart row 8 (10; 10; 12; 12) has been completed, thus ending with a WS row.

Keeping chart correct, dec 1 st at end of next and every foll 4th row until 44 (47; 50; 53; 56) sts rem.

Complete to match Left Front, reversing shapings.

SLEEVES (MAKE TWO)
Using 2³/₄mm (no 12/US 2) needles, cast on 47 (47; 51; 51; 55) sts with yarn A.

Work hem
Work 8 rows in moss st (seed st) as given for Back.

Begin chart pattern
Change to 3¹/₄mm (no 10/US 3) needles. Using the intarsia technique described in the basic information (see page 10), joining in and breaking off yarns as required, reading odd numbered K rows from right to left and even numbered P rows from left to right, beg with a K row, work in patt from sleeve chart, which is worked entirely in st st, until chart row 8 has been completed, thus ending with a WS row.

CHAMPAGNE PLEASE v-neck cardigan

Keeping chart correct, taking all inc sts into patt, inc 1 st at each end of next and every foll 8th row until 65 (75; 67; 77; 71) sts.

1st, 3rd, 4th and 5th sizes only

Keeping chart correct, taking all inc sts into patt, inc 1 st at each end of every foll 10th row to 73 (77; 79; 81) sts.

Shape top

Keeping chart correct, cast off (bind off) 4 (4; 5; 5; 6) sts at beg of next 2 rows. 65 (67; 67; 69; 69) sts.

Dec 1 st at each end of next 3 rows, then on foll 4 alt (other) rows. 51 (53; 53; 55; 55) sts. Cont without shaping for 3 further rows, thus ending with WS row.

Dec 1 st at each end of next and every foll 4th row until 41 (45; 43; 47; 45) sts rem, then on every foll alt (other) row until 35 sts rem.

Dec 1 st at each end on next 3 rows. 29 sts.

Cast off (bind off) 4 sts at beg of next 2 rows. Cast off (bind off) rem 21 sts.

FINISHING

Press all pieces on WS with a warm iron over a damp cloth. Join shoulder seams using backstitch or mattress stitch.

Button border

With RS facing, slip 5 sts left on stitch holder for button border onto 2³/₄mm (no 12/US 2) needles and rejoin yarn A.

Cont in moss st (seed st) as set until border, when slightly stretched, fits up Left Front neck edge to shoulder and then across to centre back neck, thus ending with WS row.

Cast off (bind off).

Slip stitch button border in place.

Mark positions for 5 buttons on this border – lowest button level with buttonhole already worked in Right Front, top button 1cm (¹/₃ in) below start of front neck shaping and rem 3 buttons evenly spaced between.

Buttonhole border

Work as for button border but rejoining yarn with WS facing and with the addition of 4 further buttonholes to correspond with positions marked for buttons worked as folls:

1st buttonhole row (RS): Work 2 sts in moss st (seed st), yrn (to make a buttonhole), work 2 tog, work 1 st in moss st (seed st). Slip-stitch buttonhole border in place. Sew buttons on to correspond with buttonholes. Sew in sleeves using backstitch or mattress stitch, matching centre of sleeves to shoulder seam. Join side and sleeve seams using backstitch or mattress stitch. See the basic information (page 13) for further finishing instructions.

Key

- ☐ A
- ⊙ B
- ⊞ C
- ⊠ D
- ⊚ E

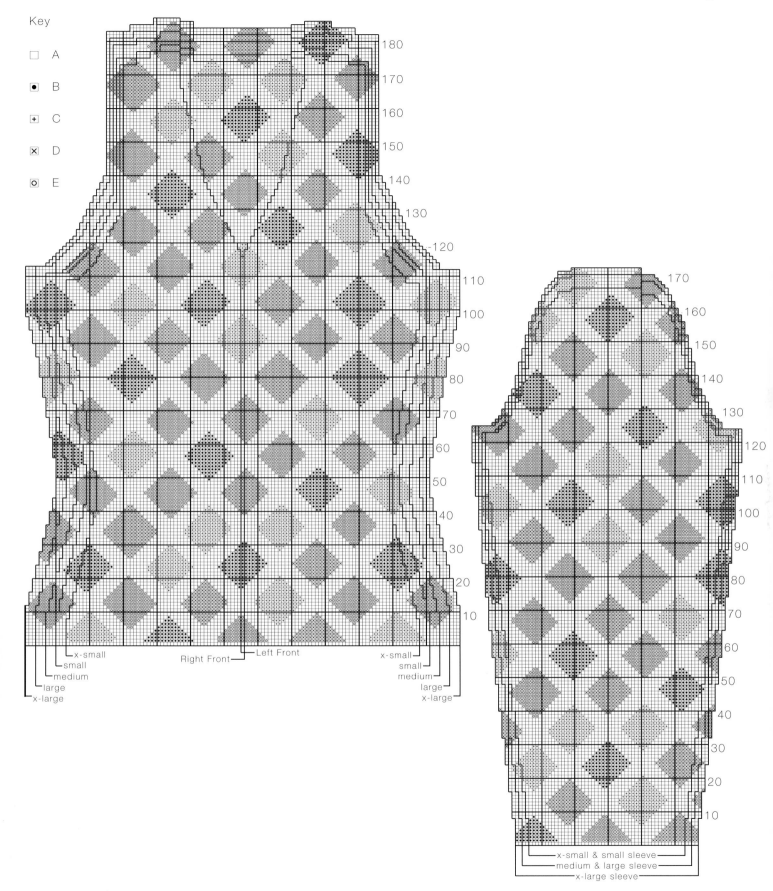

x-small
small
medium
large
x-large

Right Front — Left Front

x-small
small
medium
large
x-large

x-small & small sleeve
medium & large sleeve
x-large sleeve

NANTUCKET collared cardigan

White-washed picket fences in front of seaside cottages, seagulls sawing against hazy blue sky, pink candyfloss from an amusement stall, sand dunes stretching into the dim distance; a refreshingly cool colour palette to work with. This garment also has a very wide body to give a loose, soft swing – like laundry caught in the wind on a washing line. Knitted in Rowan True 4 ply Botany, the garment is worked from side to side rather than bottom to top, knitting bands of colour rather than having to juggle several colours across the row.

Yarn
Rowan True 4 ply Botany

			Small	Medium	Large/Extra-large
To fit up to bust			157cm (62 in)	173cm (68 in)	188cm (74 in)
A	Rowan True 4 ply Botany	lavender (580)	4	5	7 x 50g
B	Rowan True 4 ply Botany	grey (577)	2	2	2 x 50g
C	Rowan True 4 ply Botany	pink (579)	2	2	2 x 50g
D	Rowan True 4 ply Botany	lime green (573)	2	2	2 x 50g
E	Rowan True 4 ply Botany	ecru (545)	2	2	2 x 50g
F	Rowan True 4 ply Botany	beige (576)	2	2	2 x 50g
G	Rowan True 4 ply Botany	pale turquoise (578)	2	2	2 x 50g

Needles
1 pair 3mm (no 11/US 2) needles

Buttons
6

Tension
29 stitches and 38 rows to 10cm (4 in) measured over patterned stocking (stockinette) stitch using 3mm (no 11/US 2) needles.

Pattern notes
All pieces are worked sideways. Back for all sizes has colours balanced at both seams. Beg and end with yarn C (B, G).

Stripe pattern
Stripe patt is worked foll chart using yarn A throughout and changing background colours for each band with rows 3–17 representing band 1, and rows 20–34 representing band 2 as folls:

Work band 1 with yarn B.
Work band 2 with yarn C.
Work band 1 with yarn D.
Work band 2 with yarn E.
Work band 1 with yarn F.
Work band 2 with yarn G.

BACK
Using 3mm (no 11/US 2) needles, cast on 168 (168, 176) sts with yarn A.

Begin chart pattern
Using the intarsia technique described in the basic information (see page 10), joining in and breaking off colours as required, reading odd numbered K rows from right to left and even numbered P rows from left to right, beg with a K row, work in patt from body chart, which is worked in st st, until chart row 2 has been completed, thus ending with a WS row.

Next row (RS): Beg with yarn C (B, G) for the background colour, work 16 st patt rep to end, thus ending with st 8 (8; 16).
Cont to foll chart in this way until 6 (7, 8) complete colour bands, then work 8 further rows of next colour band, thus ending with rows 10 or 26.

Shape back neck
Next row (RS): Dec 1 st at neck edge, work in patt to end.
Cont to dec 1 st at neck edge on foll 4 rows. 163 (163; 171) sts.
Cont without shaping until 3 further colour bands have been completed, then work until row 4 or 22 of next colour band has been completed, thus ending with a WS row.
Inc 1 st at neck edge on foll 5 rows. 168 (168; 176) sts.
Cont without shaping in patt as before until Back measures approx 77.5 (86; 95) cm or 30½ (34; 37½) in from beg and 17 colour bands have been completed.
Cast off (bind off).

LEFT FRONT
Using 3mm (no 11/US 2) needles, cast on 168 (168, 176) sts with yarn A.

Beg with a K row, work 2 rows in st st.

Begin chart pattern
Beg with yarn B (G, F) work in colour patt as given for Back up to same row for beg of neck shaping.

Shape front neck
Next row (RS): Cast off (bind off) 9 sts, work in patt to end.
Cast off (bind off) 2 sts from neck edge every alt (other) row 6 times.
Dec 1 st at neck edge on every 3rd row 4 times. 143 (143; 151) sts.
Cont without shaping until 8 (9; 10) colours bands have been completed.

Work front band
Work 1 solid colour band without chevrons in next sequential colour for front band.
Change to yarn A.
Work 1 row in st st.
Next row (RS): P to end to form hemline ridge.

Work 14 rows in st st.
Cast off (bind off).

RIGHT FRONT
Using 3mm (no 11/US 2) needles, cast on
143 (143: 151) sts with yarn A.
Beg with a K row, work 6 rows in st st.
1st buttonhole row (RS): K5, cast off (bind
off) 3 sts, K until 23 sts from last cast off
(bind off) on right-hand needle, * cast off
(bind off) 3 sts, K until 22 (22: 24) sts from
cast-off (bind-off) on right-hand needle, rep
from * 3 further times, cast off (bind off) 3
sts, K to end.
2nd buttonhole row: P across row, casting
on sts over those cast off (bound off) on
previous row.
Beg with a K row, work 6 rows in st st.
Next row (RS): P to end to form hemline
ridge.
Beg with yarn F for first colour band, work in
colour bands as given for Left Front, working
6 further buttonholes at centre of band to
correspond to front one and reversing
shapings at neck edge by casting on and inc
instead of casting off (binding off) and dec.

SLEEVES (MAKE TWO)
Using 3mm (no 11/US 2) needles, cast on 2
sts with yarn G.
Beg with a K row, work 12 rows in st st.
Beg with yarn F for first colour band, cont in
stripe sequence but in reverse and AT THE
SAME TIME shape seam edge of sleeve by
casting on at beg of P rows, 2 sts 13 times,
3 sts 10 times, 4 sts once. 62 sts.
Cont in colour bands until 5 (5: 6) complete

patt bands have been completed at cuff edge (end of RS rows is cuff edge) and cuff measures 23 (23; 26.5) cm or 9 (9; 10½) in. Cast off (bind off) 4 sts from cuff edge on next row, 3 sts on foll 10 rows and 2 sts on foll 14 rows.

FINISHING
Press all pieces on WS with a warm iron over a damp cloth.

Work hems
Using 3mm (no 11/US 2) needles, with yarn A, pick up and K approx 15 sts across each colour band along lower back edge.

Next row (WS): K to end to form hemline ridge.

Beg with a K row, work 14 rows in st st.

Cast off (bind off).

Work front hems and sleeve cuff hems in the same way.

Sew shoulder seams.

Place markers at 24 (24: 26) cm or 9½ (9½: 10¼) in down from shoulders.

Sew sleeves to armholes between markers. Sew front band hems to WS and reinforce buttonholes. Turn up lower hems and sew to WS, mitering at front corners. Sew sleeve hems to WS. Sew side and sleeve seams. Sew on buttons.

Collar
With yarn A, beg and end at centre of front bands, pick up and K 102 sts evenly around neck edge.

Work in garter st for 6.5cm (2½ in).

Inc 1 st at each side every alt (other) row by M1 at 2 sts from each end.

Cast off (bind off).

Key

■ A

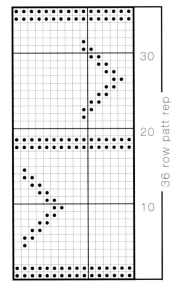

RICE PAPER round-neck cardigan

Japan has the most exquisite selection of fine papers used for origami and gift-wrapping. Just as Britain and the United States have yarn and patchwork fabric shops, Japan has shops specializing in paper. There is always a wide selection of tissue paper of fine textures and tones to be found, many with the appearance of being handmade. In one of my workshops, a student gave me a selection of papers so fine they were translucent. Taking the soft, calm palette created by these papers, I conjured up this design. The design may look as if there are many colour changes but it is, in fact, quite simple to make. For the creamy background I took lengths of different shades of colour, knotted them together to make a ball and knitted away. I then dropped in flat areas of colour with a cross running through them. The cross is variegated, too, because it is made from the same knotted background yarns. I borrowed Kaffe's idea for the magic ball method used for his Persian Poppy design in *Glorious Knitting*.

Yarn

Rowan Cotton Glacé, Rowan Fine Cotton Chenille and Rowan 4-ply Cotton

			Small 86cm (34 in)	Medium 91cm (36 in)	Large/Extra-large 97cm (38 in)
To fit up to bust					
A	Rowan Cotton Glacé	dark beige (791)	2	2	2 x 50g
B	Rowan Cotton Glacé	pale beige (730)	4	4	4 x 50g
C	Rowan Cotton Glacé	pink (724)	1	1	1 x 50g
D	Rowan Cotton Glacé	ecru (725)	1	1	1 x 50g
E	Rowan Cotton Glacé	yellow-green (780)	1	1	1 x 50g
F	Rowan 4-ply Cotton	natural (112)	1	1	1 x 50g
G	Rowan 4-ply Cotton	pale blue-green (121)	1	1	1 x 50g
H	Rowan Fine Cotton Chenille	fawn (415)	1	1	1 x 50g
J	Rowan Fine Cotton Chenille	ecru (414)	1	1	1 x 50g
L	Rowan Cotton Glacé	pale pink (747)	1	1	1 x 50g
M	Rowan Fine Cotton Chenille	green (411)	1	1	2 x 50g
N	Rowan Cotton Glacé	pink-purple (723)	1	1	1 x 50g
P	Rowan Cotton Glacé	dusky rose (793)	1	1	2 x 50g
R	Rowan Cotton Glacé	terracotta (786)	1	2	2 x 50g
S	Rowan Cotton Glacé	green-blue (748)	2	2	2 x 50g

Needles

1 pair 2³/₄mm (no 12/US 2) needles
1 pair 3¹/₄mm (no 10/US 3) needles
stitch holder

Buttons

6

Tension

23 stitches and 32 rows to 10cm (4 in) measured over patterned stocking (stockinette) stitch using 3¹/₄mm (no 10/US 3) needles.

Pattern tip

The design on this garment consists of squares of colour, each overlaid with a diagonal cross, worked on a randomly striped background. The chart reflects random stripes shown in photograph. To create totally random stripes, cut random lengths of all yarns used for striped background and wind them into one ball of yarn. Use this ball of yarn for background areas and the cross overlaid on each solid coloured square.

BACK

Using 2³/₄mm (no 12/US 2) needles, cast on 122 (128: 134) sts with yarn B.
Work 7 rows in garter st, thus ending with a RS row.
Next row (WS): K6, slip these 6 sts on to stitch holder for Left Back side vent edging, M1, K to last 6 sts, M1, turn, slipping last 6 sts on to another stitch holder for Right Back side vent edging. 112 (118: 124) sts.

Begin chart pattern

Change to 3¹/₄mm (no 10/US 3) needles.

Using a combination of the intarsia and Fair Isle techniques described in the basic information (see pages 10–11), joining in and breaking off yarns and knitting in yarns as required, reading odd numbered K rows from right to left and even numbered P rows from left to right, beg with a K row, work in patt from body chart, which is worked entirely in st st, until chart row 38 (40: 42) has been completed, thus ending with a WS row.
Taking all cast-on sts into patt, cast on 5 sts at beg of next 2 rows. 122 (128: 134) sts.

Cont without shaping until chart row 132 (140: 148) has been completed, thus ending with a WS row.

Shape armholes

Keeping chart correct, cast off (bind off) 4 sts at beg of next 2 rows. 114 (120: 126) sts.
Dec 1 st at each end on next 5 rows, then on every foll alt (other) row until 98 (104: 110) sts rem.
Cont without shaping until chart row 212 (220: 228) has been completed, thus ending with a WS row.

Shape shoulders and back neck

Cast off (bind off) 10 (11: 12) sts at beg of next 2 rows. 78 (82: 86) sts.

Divide for neck shaping on next row as folls:

Next row (RS): Cast off (bind off) 11 (12: 13) sts, work in patt until 15 (16: 17) sts on right-hand needle, turn, leaving rem sts on stitch holder.

Work each side of neck separately.

Next row: Cast off (bind off) 4 sts, work in patt to end. 11 (12: 13) sts.

Cast off (bind off) rem 11 (12: 13) sts.

With RS facing, rejoin yarn to rem sts, cast off centre 26 sts, work in patt to end.

Complete to match first side, reversing shapings.

POCKET LININGS (MAKE TWO)

Using 3¼mm (no 10/US 3) needles, cast on 28 sts with yarn B.

Beg with a K row, work 40 rows in st st.

Leave all sts on stitch holder.

LEFT FRONT

Using 2¾mm (no 12/US 2) needles, cast on 69 (72: 75) sts with yarn B.

Work 7 rows in garter st, thus ending with a RS row.

Next row (WS): K8, slip these 8 sts on to stitch holder for button band, M1, K to last 6 sts, M1, turn, slipping last 6 sts on to another stitch holder for side vent edging. 57 (60: 63) sts.

Begin chart pattern

Change to 3¼mm (no 10/US 3) needles.

Using a combination of the intarsia and Fair Isle techniques described in the basic information (see pages 10–11), joining in and breaking off yarns and knitting in yarns as required, reading odd numbered K rows from right to left and even numbered P rows from left to right, beg with a K row, work in patt from left front chart, which is worked entirely in st st, until chart row 38 (40: 42) has been completed, thus ending with a WS row.

Next row: Taking cast-on sts into patt, cast on 5 sts, work in patt to end. 62 (65: 68) sts.

Cont without shaping until chart row 52 (54: 56) has been completed, thus ending with a WS row.

Place pocket

Keeping chart correct, join in pocket lining on next row as folls:

Next row (RS): Work 16 (17: 18) sts in patt, slip next 28 sts onto stitch holder, in place of these sts work in patt across 28 sts from first

pocket lining, work in patt to end.

Cont without shaping until chart row 132 (140: 148) has been completed, thus ending with a WS row.

Shape armhole

Next row: Cast off (bind off) 4 sts, work in patt to end. 58 (61: 64) sts.

Cont without shaping for 1 further row.

Dec 1 st at armhole edge on next 5 rows, then on every foll alt (other) row until 50 (53: 56) sts rem.

Cont without shaping until chart row 191 (199: 207) has been completed, thus ending with a RS row.

Shape neck

Cast off (bind off) 4 sts at beg of next and foll alt (other) row. 42 (45: 48) sts.

Dec 1 st at neck edge on next 7 rows then on every foll alt (other) row until 33 (36: 39) sts rem.

Cont without shaping for 3 further rows.

Dec 1 st at neck edge of next row. 32 (35: 38) sts.

Cont without shaping for 3 further rows, thus ending with chart row 212 (220: 228) and a WS row.

Shape shoulder

Cast off (bind-off) 10 (11: 12) sts at beg of next row then 11 (12: 13) sts at beg of foll alt (other) row. 11 (12: 13) sts.

Cont without shaping for 1 further row.

Cast off (bind off) rem 11 (12: 13) sts.

RIGHT FRONT

Using 2³/₄mm (no 12/US 2) needles, cast on 69 (72: 75) sts with yarn B.

Work 7 rows in garter st, thus ending with a RS row.

Next row (WS): K6, slip these 6 sts onto stitch holder for side vent edging, M1, K to last 8 sts, M1, turn, slipping last 8 sts onto another stitch holder for buttonhole band. 57 (60: 63) sts.

Begin chart pattern

Change to 3¼mm (no 10/US 3) needles. Using a combination of the intarsia and Fair Isle techniques described in the basic information (see pages 10–11), joining in and breaking off yarns and knitting in yarns as required, reading odd numbered K rows from right to left and even numbered P rows from left to right, beg with a K row, work in patt from right front chart, which is worked entirely in st st, until chart row 39 (41: 43) has been completed, thus ending with a RS row.

Next row: Taking cast-on sts into patt, cast on 5 sts, work in patt to end. 62 (65: 68) sts. Cont without shaping until chart row 52 (54: 56) has been completed, thus ending with a WS row.

Place pocket

Keeping chart correct, join in pocket lining on next row as folls:

Next row (RS): Work 18 (20: 22) sts in patt, slip next 28 sts onto stitch holder, in place of these sts work in patt across 28 sts from second pocket lining, work in patt to end. Complete to match Left Front, reversing all shapings.

SLEEVES (MAKE TWO)

Using 2³/₄mm (no 12/US 2) needles, cast on 52 sts with yarn B.

Work 8 rows in garter st, thus ending with a WS row.

Begin chart pattern

Change to 3¼mm (no 10/US 3) needles. Using a combination of the intarsia and Fair Isle techniques described in the basic information (see pages 10–11), joining in and breaking off yarns and knitting in yarns as required, reading odd numbered K rows from right to left and even numbered P rows from left to right, beg with a K row, work in patt from sleeve chart, which is worked entirely in st st, taking all inc sts into patt, inc 1 st at each end of 3rd row and every foll 4th row

until 110 sts then on every foll 6th row until 116 sts.

Cont without further shaping until chart row 142 has been completed, thus ending with a WS row.

Shape top

Keeping chart correct, cast off (bind off) 4 sts at beg of next 2 rows. 108 sts.

Dec 1 st at each end of next and foll 2 alt (other) rows, thus ending with a RS row. 102 sts.

Dec 1 st at each end of next 5 rows. 92 sts. Cast off (bind off) rem 92 sts loosely and evenly.

FINISHING

Press all pieces on WS with a warm iron over a damp cloth. Join both shoulder seams using backstitch or mattress stitch.

Side vent edgings (all 4 alike)

With RS facing for Left Back and Right Front and with WS facing for Right Back and Left Front, slip 6 sts on stitch holder for side vent edgings on 2³/₄mm (no 12/US 2) needles and rejoin yarn B.

Cont in garter st until edging, when slightly stretched, fits up side vent to cast on sts, thus ending with a WS row.

Cast off (bind off) loosely and evenly.

Slip-stitch edging in place along sides and tops.

Pocket tops (both alike)

With RS facing, slip 28 sts on stitch holder for pocket tops onto 2³/₄mm (no 12/US 2) needles and rejoin yarn B.

K 5 rows.

Cast off (bind off) knitwise.

Button band

With RS facing, slip 8 sts on Left Front stitch holder for button band on 2³/₄mm (no 12/US 2) needles and rejoin yarn B.

Cont in garter st until button band, when slightly stretched, fits up Left Front opening edge to neck shaping, thus ending with a WS row.

Cast off (bind off) loosely and evenly.

Slip-stitch button band in place.

Mark positions for 5 buttons on this band, the first to come level with top of pocket, the last 1.5cm (¹/₂ in) below neck, and rem spaced evenly between.

Buttonhole band

With RS facing, slip 8 sts on Right Front stitch holder for button band on 2³/₄mm (no 12/

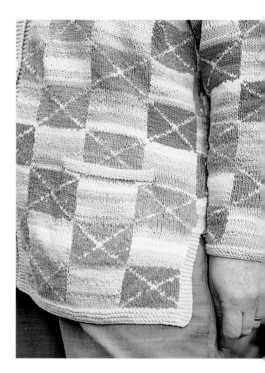

US 2) needles and rejoin yarn B.

Work to match button band, with the addition of 5 buttonholes worked to correspond with positions marked for buttons as folls:

1st buttonhole row (RS): K3, (yfwd) twice (to make a st – drop one of these loops on next row), K2tog, K3.

Slip-stitch buttonhole band in place.

Collar

With RS facing, using 2³/₄mm (no 12/US 2) needles with yarn B, starting midway across top of buttonhole band, pick up and K 33 sts up Right Front neck, 34 sts across Back neck, and 33 sts down Left Front neck, ending midway across top of button band. 100 sts.

K 5 rows, thus ending with a WS row.

Next row (RS) (dec): K2, K2tog, K to last 4 sts, K2tog tbl, K2.

K 1 row.

Rep last 2 rows 4 further times and then first of these 2 rows (the dec row) again. 88 sts. Cast off (bind off) knitwise.

Sew in sleeves using backstitch or mattress stitch, matching centre of sleeves to shoulder seam. Join side seams and sleeve seams using backstitch or mattress stitch. Catch down pocket linings on WS. See the basic information (page 13) for further finishing instructions.

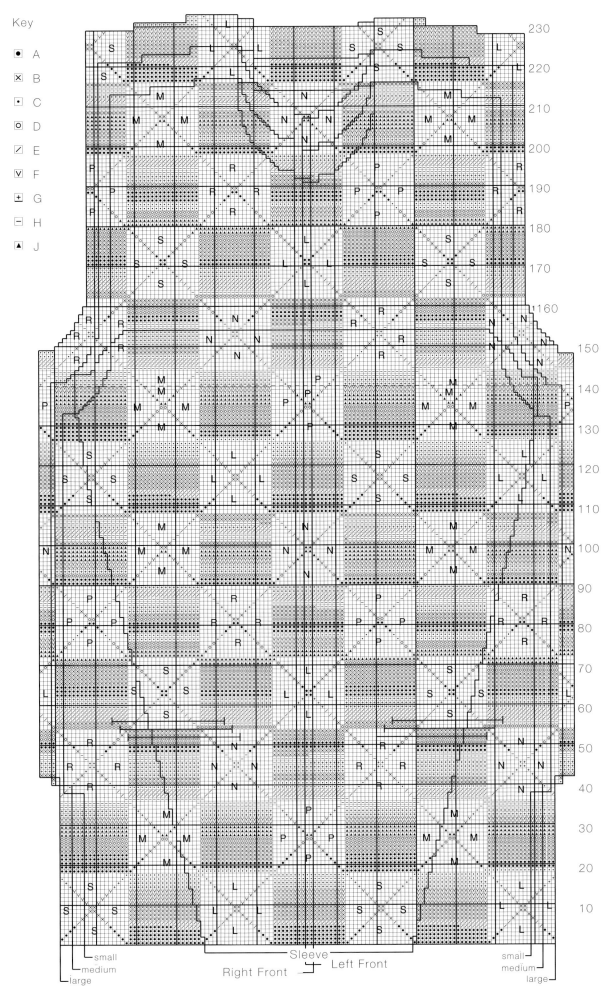

Key

- ● A
- ⊠ B
- ⊡ C
- ⊙ D
- ⊘ E
- ⋁ F
- ⊞ G
- ⊟ H
- ▲ J

TRELLIS crewneck sweater

I have been fortunate to visit South Africa several times and work with craftsmen and artists from the townships. They bring to their work a freshness and instinctive nature, which can be sometimes spoiled by training. There is a definite element of humour, expression and passion in their work – baskets woven from multi-coloured telephone wire, scavenged remnants of fabric made into patchworks, even the walls of their corrugated tin homes lined with repeats of commercial labels. Their ingenuity for using society's cast-offs is astounding. South Africa has to be the most inspiring country for me. The free sense of design and expression is so strong, playful and pleasing, and a thrill to my imagination. A painting marked out on a piece of hessian cloth with mud and a stick inspired Trellis. The colours of the painting were cold dark brown on a pale cloth background but I have chosen a softer, more wearable palette to work with, streaking the backgrounds with touches of steely grey and dusty terracotta to add texture to the solid areas of the design.

Yarn

Rowan DK Tweed

			Small	Medium	Large/Extra-large
To fit up to chest			81–86.5cm (32–34 in)	91.5–96.5cm (36–38 in)	102–107cm (40–42 in)
A	Rowan DK Tweed	pale grey/green (851)	1	1	1 x 50g
B	Rowan DK Tweed	oatmeal (850)	9	9	9 x 50g
C	Rowan DK Tweed	mid-brown (853)	6	6	7 x 50g
D	Rowan DK Tweed	dark grey (852)	2	2	2 x 50g
E	Rowan DK Tweed	rust (864)	2	2	2 x 50g

Needles

1 pair 3¼mm (no 10/US 3) needles
1 pair 3¾mm (no 9/US 5) needles
1 pair 4mm (no 8/US 6) needles
stitch holder

Tension

21 stitches and 29 rows to 10cm (4 in) measured over patterned stocking (stockinette) stitch using 4mm (no 8/US 6) needles.

BACK

Using 3¾mm (no 9/US 5) needles, cast on 65 (69; 73) sts with yarn B and then 65 (69; 73) sts with yarn C. 130 (138; 146) sts.

Work rib

Using the intarsia technique described in the basic information (see page 10), joining in and breaking off colours as required, work as folls:

Row 1 (RS): Using yarn C P1, [K2, P2] 16 (17; 18) times, using yarn B [K2, P2] 16 (17; 18) times, K1.

Row 2: Using yarn B P1, [K2, P2] 16 (17; 18) times, using yarn C [K2, P2] 16 (17; 18) times, K1.

Rep last 2 rows 3 further times.

Begin chart pattern

Change to 4mm (no 8/US 6) needles.

Using a mixture of the intarsia and Fair Isle techniques described in the basic information (see pages 10–11), joining in and breaking off colours as required, reading odd numbered K rows from left to right and even numbered P rows from right to left, beg with a K row, work in patt from body chart, which is worked entirely in st st, until chart row 106 has been completed, thus ending with a WS row.

Shape armholes

Keeping chart correct, cast off (bind off) 6 sts at beg of next 2 rows. 118 (126; 134) sts.

Cont without shaping until chart row 182 has been completed, thus ending with a WS row.

Shape shoulders and back neck

Keeping chart correct, cast off (bind off) 12 (13; 14) sts at beg of next 2 rows. 94 (100; 106) sts.

Divide for neck shaping on next row as folls:

Next row (RS): Cast off (bind off) 12 (13; 14) sts, work in patt until 15 (17; 19) sts on right-hand needle, turn, leaving rem sts on stitch holder.

Work each side of neck separately.

Next row: Cast off (bind off) 4 sts, work in patt to end. 11 (13; 15) sts.

Cast off (bind off) rem 11 (13; 15) sts.

With RS facing, rejoin yarn to rem sts on stitch holder, cast off (bind off) centre 40 sts for neckband, work in patt to end.

Complete to match first side, reversing shapings.

FRONT

Using 3¾mm (no 9/US 5) needles cast on 65 (69; 73) sts using yarn C and then 65 (69; 73) sts using yarn B. 130 (138; 146) sts.

Work rib

Using the intarsia technique described in the basic information (see page 10), joining in and breaking off colours as required, work as folls:

Row 1 (RS): Using yarn B P1, [K2, P2] 16 (17; 18) times, using yarn C [K2, P2] 16 (17; 18) times, K1.

Row 2: Using yarn C P1, [K2, P2] 16 (17; 18) times, using yarn B [K2, P2] 16 (17; 18) times, K1.

Rep last 2 rows 3 further times.

Begin chart pattern

Change to 4mm (no 8/US 6) needles.

Using a mixture of the intarsia and Fair Isle techniques described in the basic information (see pages 10–11), joining in and breaking off colours as required, reading odd numbered K rows from right to left and even numbered P rows from left to right, beg with a K row, work in patt from body chart, which is worked entirely in st st, until chart row 106 has been completed, thus ending with a WS row.

Shape armholes

Keeping chart correct, cast off (bind off) 6 sts at beg of next 2 rows. 118 (126; 134) sts.
Cont wihtout shaping until chart row 164 has been completed, thus ending with a WS row.

Shape neck

Divide for neck shaping on next row as folls:
Next row (RS): Work in patt until 49 (53; 57) sts on right-hand needle, turn, leaving rem sts on stitch holder.
Work each side of neck separately.
Keeping chart correct, cast off (bind off) 4 sts at beg of next row. 45 (49; 53) sts.
Dec 1 st at neck edge on next 7 rows, then on foll 2 alt (other) rows. 36 (40; 44) sts.
Cont without shaping for 3 further rows.
Dec 1 st at neck edge on next row. 35 (39; 43) sts.
Cont without shaping for 1 further row, thus ending with chart row 182.

Shape shoulder

Keeping chart correct, cast off (bind off) 12

(13; 14) sts at beg of next and foll alt row. 11 (13; 15) sts.
Cont without shaping for 1 further row.
Cast off (bind off) rem 11 (13; 15) sts.
With RS facing, rejoin yarn to rem sts on stitch holder, cast off (bind off) centre 20 sts for neckband, work in patt to end.
Complete to match first side, reversing shapings.

LEFT SLEEVE

Using 3³⁄₄mm (no 9/US 5) needles, cast on 58 sts with yarn C.
Row 1 (RS): K2, * P2, K2, rep from * to end.
Row 2: P2, * K2, P2, rep from * to end.
Rep last 2 rows 3 further times.

Begin chart pattern

Change to 4mm (no 8/US 6) needles.
Using a mixture of the intarsia and Fair Isle techniques described in the basic information (see pages 10–11), joining in and breaking off colours as required, reading odd numbered K rows from right to left and even numbered P rows from left to right, beg with a K row, work in patt from left sleeve chart, which is worked entirely in st st, taking all inc sts into patt, inc 1 st at each end of chart row 3 and every foll 4th row until 98 sts, then on every foll 6th row

until 112 sts.
Cont without shaping until chart row 140 has been completed, thus ending with a WS row.
Cast off (bind off) loosely and evenly.

RIGHT SLEEVE

Work as given for Left Sleeve but using yarn B for first 8 rows and then foll right sleeve chart.

FINISHING

Press all pieces on WS with a warm iron over a damp cloth. Join right shoulder seam using backstitch or mattress stitch.

Neckband

With RS facing, using 3¹⁄₄mm (no 10/US 3) needles with yarn C, pick up and K 21 sts down Left Front neck, 20 sts across Front neck, 21 sts up Right Front neck and 48 sts across Back neck. 110 sts.
Work 8 rows in rib as given for sleeves.
Cast off (bind off) loosely and evenly in rib.
Join left shoulder seam using backstitch or mattress stitch. Sew in sleeves using backstitch or mattress stitch, matching centre of sleeves to shoulder seam. Join side and sleeve seams. See the basic information (page 13) for further finishing instructions.

TRELLIS crewneck sweater

Key

☒ A

☐ B

⊡ C

☒ D

⊟ E

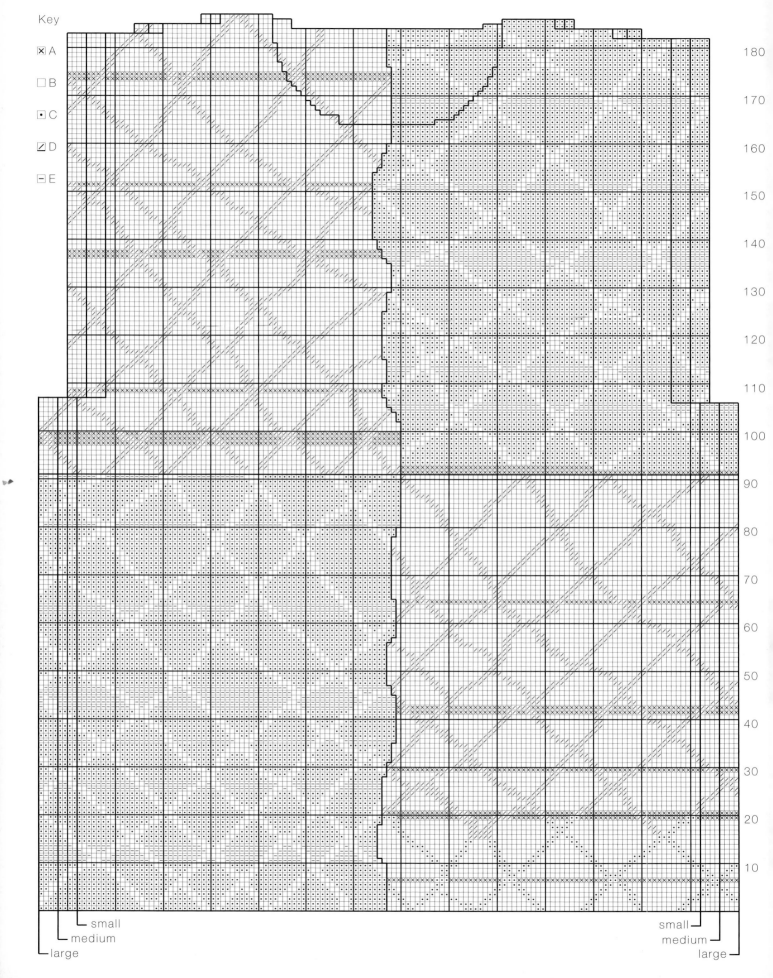

small

medium

large

small

medium

large

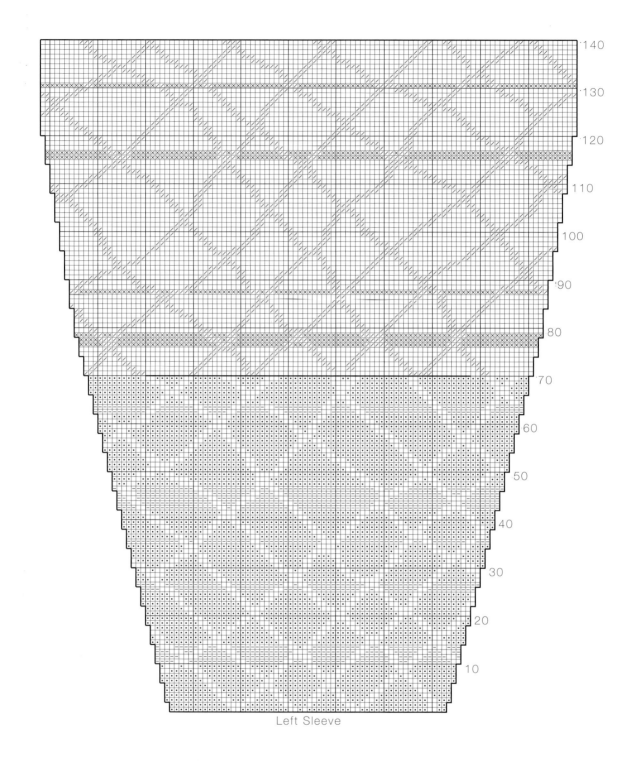

Left Sleeve

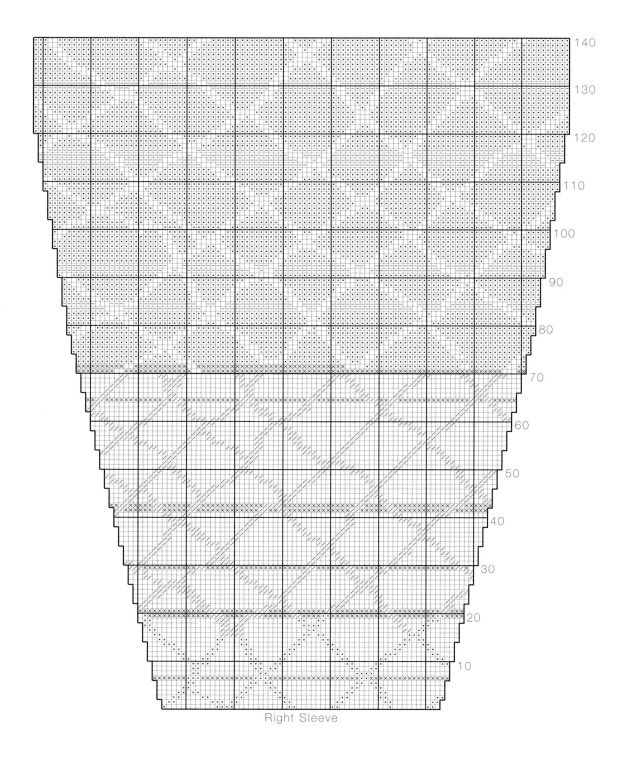

Right Sleeve

GAME BOARD round-neck cardigan

I suppose to a lot of people, the square is the most pedestrian of forms. But neatly arranged in a grid, its design possibilities are legion. Perfect examples are seen in patchwork, crochet blankets, decorative tiles and mosaics. An exciting example of a chequerboard can be seen on a church in North London; indeed, the whole building is built in a bold chequerboard pattern of flint stone in shades of mottled fawn and soft blue-black. This structure, together with its very English colouring, served as the perfect inspiration for this design. Using Rowan DK Soft and Rowan Felted Tweed, I chose to design a woman's jacket with a soft, loose swing. The design knits up beautifully as a man's crewneck sweater too (see pages 90–91).

Yarn
Rowan DK Soft and Rowan Felted Tweed

			Small 81–86cm (32–34 in)	Medium 91cm (36 in)	Large/Extra-large 97–102cm (38–40 in)
To fit up to bust					
A	Rowan DK Soft	dark grey (169)	8	8	9 x 50g
B	Rowan DK Soft	grey (173)	2	2	2 x 50g
C	Rowan Felted Tweed	mid-grey (140)	3	3	3 x 50g
D	Rowan Felted Tweed	blue-grey (141)	4	4	4 x 50g
E	Rowan DK Soft	purple (165)	2	2	2 x 50g
F	Rowan DK Soft	blue-grey (174)	2	2	2 x 50g
G	Rowan Felted Tweed	green-gold (138)	2	2	3 x 50g
H	Rowan DK Soft	sage green (175)	2	2	3 x 50g
J	Rowan Felted Tweed	gold (136)	2	2	2 x 50g
L	Rowan Felted Tweed	rose pink (137)	2	2	3 x 50g

Needles
1 pair 3¼mm (no 10/US 3) needles
1 pair 3¾mm (no 9/US 5) needles
stitch holder

Buttons
7

Tension
23 stitches and 32 rows to 10cm (4 in) measured over patterned stocking (stockinette) stitch using 3¾mm (no 9/US 5) needles.

BACK
Using 3¼mm (no 10/US 3) needles, cast on 210 (220: 230) sts with yarn D.
Work hem
Work 10 rows in garter st.
Begin chart pattern
Change to 3¾mm (no 9/US 5) needles.
Using the intarsia technique described in the basic information (see page 10), joining in and breaking off colours as required, reading odd numbered K rows from right to left and even numbered P rows from left to right, beg with a K row, work in patt foll body chart for woman's cardigan, which is worked entirely in st st, until chart row 196 (200: 204) has been completed, thus ending with a WS row.
Shape shoulders and back neck
Keeping chart correct, cast off (bind off) 17 (18: 19) sts at beg of next 6 rows. 108 (112: 116) sts.
Divide for neck shaping on next row as folls:

Next row (RS): Cast off (bind off) 17 (18: 19) sts, work in patt until 21 (22: 23) sts on right-hand needle, turn, leaving rem sts on stitch holder.
Work each side of neck separately.
Next row: Cast off (bind off) 4 sts, work in patt to end.
Cast off (bind off) rem 17 (18: 19) sts.
With RS facing, rejoin yarn to rem sts, cast off (bind off) centre 32 sts, work in patt to end.
Complete to match first side, reversing shapings.

LEFT FRONT
Using 3¼mm (no 10/US 3) needles, cast on 110 (115: 120) sts with yarn D.
Work hem
Work 10 rows in garter st.
Begin chart pattern
Change to 3¾mm (no 9/US 5) needles.
Using the intarsia technique described in the basic information (see page 10), joining in and breaking off colours as required, reading odd numbered K rows from right to left and even numbered P rows from left to right, beg with a K row, work in patt foll body chart for woman's cardigan, which is worked entirely in st st, until chart row 175 (179: 183) has been completed, thus ending with a RS row.
Shape neck
Next row (WS): Keeping chart correct, cast off (bind off) 15 sts, work in patt to end. 95 (100: 105) sts.
Dec 1 st at neck edge on next 5 rows, then on foll 4 alt (other) rows, then on foll 4th row. 85 (90: 95) sts.
Work without shaping for a further 3 rows until chart row 196 (200: 204) has been completed, thus ending with a WS row.
Shape shoulder
Cast off (bind off) 17 (18: 19) sts at beg of next and foll 3 alt (other) rows.
Work without shaping for 1 further row.
Cast off (bind off) rem 17 (18: 19) sts.

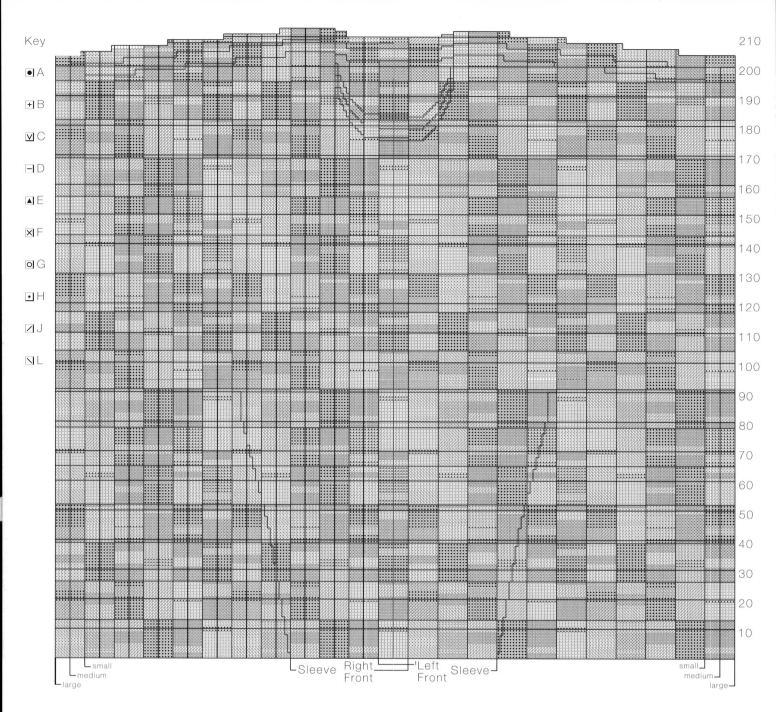

Key
- ● A
- ⊞ B
- ☑ C
- ⊟ D
- ◨ E
- ☒ F
- ◎ G
- ⊡ H
- ◩ J
- ◤ L

210
200
190
180
170
160
150
140
130
120
110
100
90
80
70
60
50
40
30
20
10

small
medium
large

Sleeve — Right Front — Left Front — Sleeve

small
medium
large

RIGHT FRONT

Work as given for Left Front, reversing all shapings and making buttonholes in chart row 17 (21: 25) and every foll 26th row as folls:

1st buttonhole row (RS): K4, cast off (bind off) 2 sts for buttonhole, K to end.

2nd buttonhole row (WS): P to last 4 sts, cast on 2 sts over those cast off (bound off) on previous row, P to end.

SLEEVES (MAKE TWO)

Using 3¼mm (no 10/US 3) needles, cast on 79 sts with yarn D.

Work hem

Work 10 rows in garter st.

Begin chart pattern

Change to 3¾mm (no 9/US 5) needles. Using the intarsia technique described in the basic information (see page 10), joining in and breaking off colours as required, reading odd numbered K rows from right to left and even numbered P rows from left to right, beg with a K row, work in patt from sleeve chart for woman's cardigan, which is worked entirely in st st, taking all inc sts into patt, inc 1 st at each end of 3rd row and then every foll 6th row until 86 sts, then on every foll 4th row until 104 sts.

Cont without shaping until chart row 90 has been completed, thus ending with a WS row.

Cast off (bind off) loosely and evenly.

FINISHING

Press all pieces on WS with a warm iron over a damp cloth. Join shoulder seams using backstitch or mattress stitch.

Left Front facing

With RS facing, using 3¼mm (no 10/US 3) needles with yarn D, pick up and K 136 (139: 142) sts evenly along Left Front opening edge.

Row 1 (WS): K to end to form foldline ridge. Beg with a K row, work 14 rows in st st. Cast off (bind off).

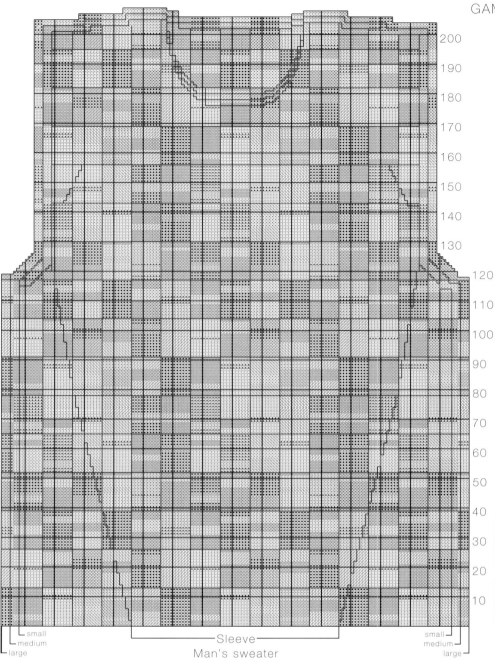

200

190

180

170

160

150

140

130

120

110

100

90

80

70

60

50

40

30

20

10

small
medium
large
───Sleeve───
Man's sweater
small
medium
large

Right Front facing

With RS facing, using 3¼mm (no 10/US 3) needles and yarn D, pick up and K 136 (139: 142) sts evenly along Right Front opening edge.

Row 1 (WS): K to end to form foldline ridge. Beg with a K row, work 14 rows in st st.

Row 6 (RS): K18 (21: 24), turn.

P 1 row on these 18 (21: 24) sts.

Break yarn.

** With RS facing, rejoin yarn to rem sts, K2tog, K17, turn.

P 1 row on these 18 sts.

Break yarn.

Rep from ** a further 5 times.

With RS facing, rejoin yarn to rem 4 sts, K2tog, K2, turn.

P 1 row on these 3 sts.

Break yarn.

With RS facing, join all sections as folls:

Row 8 (RS): K17 (20: 23) sts, inc in next st, * K17, inc in next st, rep from * a further 5 times, K rem 3 sts.

Beg with a P row, work a further 6 rows in st st.

Cast off (bind off).

Fold facing onto WS along foldline ridge and slip-stitch into position. Oversew double buttonholes.

Neckband

With RS facing, using 3¼mm (no 10/US 3)

needles with yarn D, pick up and K 38 sts up Right Front neck, 40 sts across Back neck, and 38 sts down Left Front neck. 116 sts.

Work 6 rows in garter st.

Cast off (bind off) knitwise on WS.

Sew in sleeves using backstitch or mattress stitch, matching centre of sleeves to shoulder seam. Join side seams and sleeve seams using backstitch or mattress stitch. Sew buttons on to correspond with buttonholes.

See the basic information (page 13) for further finishing instructions.

GAME BOARD crewneck sweater

Yarn

Rowan DK Soft and Rowan Felted Tweed

				Small	Medium	Large
	To fit chest			97–102cm (38–40 in)	102–107cm (40–42 in)	107–112cm (42–44 in)
A	Rowan DK Soft	dark grey (169)		2	3	3 x 50g
B	Rowan DK Soft	grey (173)		2	2	2 x 50g
C	Rowan Felted Tweed	mid-grey (140)		2	2	2 x 50g
D	Rowan Felted Tweed	blue-grey (141)		2	2	2 x 50g
E	Rowan DK Soft	purple (165)		2	2	2 x 50g
F	Rowan DK Soft	blue-grey (174)		2	2	2 x 50g
G	Rowan Felted Tweed	green-gold (138)		2	2	2 x 50g
H	Rowan DK Soft	sage green (175)		2	2	2 x 50g
J	Rowan Felted Tweed	gold (136)		2	2	2 x 50g
L	Rowan Felted Tweed	rose pink (137)		2	2	2 x 50g

Needles

1 pair 3¼mm (no 10/US 3) needles
1 pair 3¾mm (no 9/US 5) needles
stitch holder

Tension

23 stitches and 32 rows to 10cm (4 in) measured over patterned stocking (stockinette) stitch using 3¾mm (no 9/US 5) needles.

BACK

Using 3¼mm (no 10/US 3) needles, cast on 146 (150: 158) sts with yarn C.

Work rib

Work 18 rows in K2, P2 rib and AT THE SAME TIME inc 0 (1: 0) st at each end of last row. 146 (152: 158) sts.

Begin chart pattern

Change to 3¾mm (no 9/US 5) needles.
Using the intarsia technique described in the basic information (see page 10), joining in and breaking off colours as required, reading odd numbered K rows from right to left and even numbered P rows from left to right, beg with a K row, work in patt foll body chart for man's sweater (see page 89), which is worked entirely in st st, until chart row 114 (116: 118) has been completed, thus ending with a WS row.

Shape armholes

Keeping chart correct, cast off (bind off) 4 sts at beg of next 2 rows. 138 (144: 150) sts.
Dec 1 st at each end of next 7 rows. 124 (130: 136) sts.
Cont without shaping until chart row 200 (202: 204) has been completed, thus ending with a WS row.

Shape shoulders and back neck

Keeping chart correct, cast off (bind off) 13 (14: 15) sts at beg of next 2 rows. 98 (102: 106) sts.
Divide for neck shaping on next row as folls:
Next row (RS): Cast off (bind off) 13 (14: 15) sts, work in patt until 17 (18: 19) sts on right-hand needle, turn, leaving rem sts on stitch holder.
Next row: Cast off (bind off) 4 sts, work in patt to end.
Cast off (bind off) rem 13 (14: 15) sts.
With RS facing, rejoin yarn to rem sts, cast off (bind off) centre 38 sts, work in patt to end.
Complete to match first side, reversing shapings.

FRONT

Work as given for Back until chart row 176 (178: 180) has been completed, thus ending with a WS row.

Shape neck

Divide for neck shaping on next row as folls:
Next row (RS): Work in patt until 52 (55: 58) sts on right-hand needle, turn, leaving rem sts on stitch holder.
Work each side of neck separately.
Next row: Keeping chart correct, cast off (bind off) 3 sts, work in patt to end. 49 (52: 55) sts.
Dec 1 st at neck edge on next 5 rows, then on foll 3 alt (other) rows, then on every foll 4th

row until 39 (42: 45) sts rem.
Cont without shaping for a further 3 rows until chart row 200 (202: 204) has been completed, thus ending with a WS row.

Shape shoulder

Keeping chart correct, cast off (bind off) 13 (14: 15) sts at beg of next and foll alt (other) row.
Cont without shaping for 1 further row.
Cast off (bind off) rem 13 (14: 15) sts.
With RS facing, rejoin yarn to rem sts, cast off (bind off) centre 20 sts, work in patt to end.
Complete to match first side, reversing shapings.

SLEEVES (MAKE TWO)

Using 3¼mm (no 10/US 3) needles, cast on 70 sts with yarn C.

Work rib

Work 18 rows in rib as given for Back.

Begin chart pattern

Change to 3¾mm (no 9/US 5) needles.
Using the intarsia technique described in the basic information (see page 10), joining in and breaking off colours as required, reading odd numbered K rows from right to left and even numbered P rows from left to right, beg with a K row, work in patt from sleeve chart for man's sweater, which is worked entirely in

st st, taking all inc sts into patt, inc 1 st at each end of 3rd row and then every foll 4th row until 110 sts, then on every foll 6th row until 124 sts.
Cont without shaping until chart row 142 has been completed, thus ending with a WS row.

Shape top
Keeping chart correct, cast off (bind off) 4 sts at beg of next 2 rows. 116 sts.
Dec 1 st at each end of next and foll 5 alt (other) rows. 104 sts.

Cont without shaping for 1 further row.
Cast off (bind off) rem 104 sts loosely and evenly.

FINISHING
Press all pieces on WS with a warm iron over a damp cloth. Join right shoulder seam using backstitch or mattress stitch.

Neckband
With RS facing, using 3¼mm (no 10/US 3) needles with yarn C, pick up and K 26 sts up

Right Front neck, 20 sts across Front neck, 26 sts down Left Front neck, and 46 sts across Back neck. 118 sts.
Work 9 rows in rib as given for Back.
Cast off (bind off) loosely and evenly in rib.
Join left shoulder seam. Sew in sleeves using back stitch or mattress stitch, matching centre of sleeves to shoulder seam. Join side seams and sleeve seams using backstitch or mattress stitch. See the basic information (page 13) for further finishing instructions.

INTERWEAVE boat-neck sweater

Stained glass in windows has always given me thoughtful pleasure because of the outlined shafts of pure sharp colour. For this strong, fresh design, I dropped pools of pure colour into an outlined blue lattice pattern, which looks like loosely woven ribbons or the canvas strapping for an un-upholstered armchair. The design lent itself to a boxy shape using a hem rather than a rib. Originally I designed this garment for *Vogue Knitting Magazine* in Rowan Silk Tweed and Rowan Designer DK and was delighted when one customer changed the blue palette to an off-white and biscuit beige, with soft chocolate brown for the outline. It looked gorgeous, so don't be afraid to re-colour the garment to suit your own taste. The wide boat neck emphasizes the geometry of the pattern and boxy shape of this garment. It is a very easy design to use if you want to make a generous garment.

Yarn

Rowan Silk Tweed and Rowan Designer DK

			Small/Medium 138cm (54 in)	Large/Extra-large 155cm (62 in)
To fit up to bust				
A	Rowan Silk Tweed	pale blue (704)	5	6 x 50g
B	Rowan Silk Tweed	mint green (702)	5	6 x 50g
C	Rowan Silk Tweed	blue (711)	2	3 x 50g
D	Rowan Silk Tweed	rust (706)	1	1 x 50g
E	Rowan Designer DK	pink (630)	1	1 x 50g
F	Rowan Designer DK	forest green (685)	1	1 x 50g
G	Rowan Designer DK	blue (642)	1	1 x 50g
H	Rowan Designer DK	purple (636)	1	1 x 50g
J	Rowan Designer DK	red (632)	1	1 x 50g
L	Rowan Designer DK	lime (635)	1	1 x 50g
M	Rowan Designer DK	dusky pink (694)	1	1 x 50g
N	Rowan Designer DK	pale blue (629)	1	1 x 50g

Needles

1 pair 4mm (no 8/US 6) needles
1 3¼mm (no 10/US 3) circular needle
stitch holder

Tension

21 stitches and 29 rows to 10cm (4 in) measured over patterned stocking (stockinette) stitch using 4mm (no 8/US 6) needles.

BACK

Using 4mm (no 8/US 6) needles, cast on 142 (160) sts with yarn A.

Work hem

Beg with a K row, work 5 rows in st st, thus ending with a RS row.

Next row (WS): K to end to form hemline ridge.

Begin chart pattern

Using the intarsia technique described in the basic information (see page 10), joining in and breaking off colours as required, reading odd numbered K rows from right to left and even numbered P rows from left to right, beg with a K row, work in patt from body chart, which is worked entirely in st st, until chart row 168 has been completed, thus ending with a WS row.
Cast off (bind off).

FRONT

Work as given for Back until work measures 53.5cm (21 in) from hemline ridge, thus ending with a WS row.

Shape shoulders and neck

Divide for neck shaping on next row as folls:
Next row (RS): Work in patt until 54 (63) sts on right-hand needle, turn, leaving rem sts on stitch holder.
Work each side of neck separately.
Cast off (bind off) 3 sts at neck edge on next 2 rows. 48 (57) sts.
Cast off (bind off) 2 sts at neck edge of foll row. 46 (55) sts.
Dec 1 st at neck edge of every alt (other) row 3 times. 43 (52) sts.
Keeping chart correct, cont without shaping until chart row 168 has been worked, thus ending with a WS row.
With RS facing, rejoin yarn to rem sts, cast off (bind off) centre 34 sts, work in patt to end.
Complete to match first side, reversing all shapings.

SLEEVES (MAKE TWO)

With 4mm (no 8/US 6) needles, cast on 58 sts with yarn A.

Beg with a K row, work 5 rows in st st, thus ending with a RS row.

Next row: K to end to form hemline ridge.
Using the intarsia technique described in the basic information (see page 10), joining in and breaking off colours as required, reading odd numbered K rows from right to left and even numbered P rows from left to right, beg with a K row, work in patt from sleeve chart, which is worked entirely in st st, taking all inc sts into patt, inc 1 st at each end of 4th and every foll 4th row until 118 sts.
Cont without shaping until chart row 134 has been worked and Sleeve measures 47cm (18½ in) from hemline ridge.
Cast off (bind off).

FINISHING

Press all pieces on WS with a warm iron over a damp cloth. Join both shoulder seams using backstitch or mattress stitch. Place markers 28.5cm (11¼ in) down from shoulder seams on Front and Back for armholes. Sew top of Sleeve between markers. Sew side and sleeve seams.

INTERWEAVE boat-neck sweater

Neckband

With RS facing, using 3¼mm (no 10/US 3)
circular needle with yarn A, pick up and K
112 sts evenly around neck edge. 112 sts.
Work 5 rounds in K2, P2 rib.
Work in st st for 5cm (2 in), thus ending with a
WS row.
Cast off (bind off) knitwise.
See the basic information (page 13) for further
finishing instructions.

Key

 A   — D   ◎ G   ⊠ L

⊞ B   ▲ E   • H   I M

⊠ C   � F   ⁄ J   ■ N

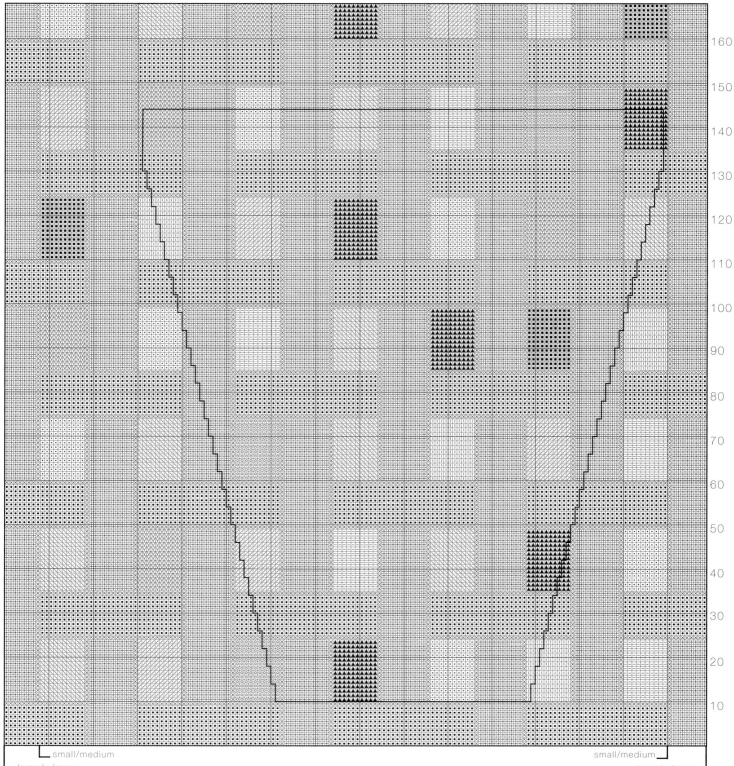

small/medium

large/x-large

small/medium

large/x-large

BANDED STRIPE crewneck sweater

What is it about stripes that is so magnetic? The markings on a zebra, a picket fence or even an accordion are fascinating. Choosing a husky, wintry palette of tweedy yarns for this stripe design, I divided the tones into equally balanced bands and then broke up the horizontal stripes by placing a wide vertical column down the middle of the design. This then gave me the opportunity to off-set the coloured bands on each side. This design is finished off with warm, toasty terracotta brown and russett red in a vertical striped rib for the botton edge, high neck band and cuffs.

Yarn

Rowan Felted Tweed and Rowan DK Tweed

One size to fit a range of sizes
To fit up to chest   132cm (52 in)

A	Rowan Felted Tweed	russett red (144)	2 x 50g
B	Rowan Felted Tweed	burgundy (134)	2 x 50g
C	Rowan DK Tweed	mulberry (865)	2 x 50g
D	Rowan DK Tweed	mid-blue (862)	2 x 50g
E	Rowan DK Tweed	stone (851)	2 x 50g
F	Rowan DK Tweed	light brown (853)	2 x 50g
G	Rowan Felted Tweed	forest green (130)	2 x 50g
H	Rowan DK Tweed	rust (864)	2 x 50g
J	Rowan DK Tweed	port (868)	2 x 50g
L	Rowan DK Tweed	sage green (866)	2 x 50g
M	Rowan Felted Tweed	green-blue (131)	2 x 50g
N	Rowan DK Tweed	dark grey (852)	2 x 50g
P	Rowan Felted Tweed	navy blue (133)	2 x 50g
R	Rowan Felted Tweed	pink-purple (139)	2 x 50g
S	Rowan Felted Tweed	blue-grey (141)	2 x 50g

Needles

1 pair 3¼mm (no 10/US 3) needles
1 pair 4mm (no 8/US 6) needles
1 3¼mm (no 10/US 3) circular needle
stitch holder

Tension

20 stitches and 29 rows to 10cm (4 in) measured over patterned stocking (stockinette) stitch using 4mm (no 8/US 6) needles.

BACK

Using 3¼mm (no 10/US 3) needles, cast on 128 sts with yarn D.

Work rib

Using the intarsia technique described in the basic information (see page 10), joining in and breaking off colours as required, work in K4, P4 rib as folls:

Row 1: * K4 with yarn A, P4 with yarn B, rep from * to end.
Row 2: * K4 with yarn B, P4 with yarn A, rep from * to end.
Rep last 2 rows 5 further times and AT THE SAME TIME inc 2 sts evenly across last row. 130 sts.

Begin chart pattern

Change to 4mm (no 8/US 6) needles.
Using the intarsia technique described in the basic information (see page 10), joining in and breaking off colours as required, reading odd numbered K rows from left to right and even numbered P rows from right to left, beg with a K row, work in patt from body chart, which is worked entirely in st st,

until chart row 98 has been completed, thus ending with a WS row.

Shape armholes

Keeping chart correct, cast off (bind off) 4 sts at beg of next 2 rows. 122 sts.
Dec 1 st at each end of next 3 rows. 116 sts.
Cont without shaping until chart row 160 has been completed, thus ending with a WS row.

Shape back neck

Divide for neck shaping on next row as folls:

Next row: Work in patt until 42 sts on right-hand needle, turn, leaving rem sts on stitch holder.
Work each side of neck separately.
Next row: Cast off (bind off) 4 sts, work in patt to end.
Cast off (bind off) rem 38 sts.
With RS facing, rejoin yarn to rem sts on stitch holder, cast off (bind off) centre 32 sts, work in patt to end.
Complete to match first side, reversing shapings.

FRONT

Work as given for Back but reading chart from right to left on odd numbered K rows and left to right on even numbered P rows until chart row 146 has been worked, ending with a WS row.

Shape front neck

Divide for neck shaping on next row as folls:

Next row: Work in patt until 47 sts on right-hand needle, turn, leaving rem sts on stitch holder.
Work each side of neck separately.
Dec 1 st at neck edge on next 6 rows and then on every alt (other) row 3 times. 38 sts.
Cont without shaping until Front has same number of rows as Back to shoulder, thus ending with a WS row.
Cast off (bind off) rem 38 sts.
With RS facing, rejoin yarn to rem sts on stitch holder, slip centre 22 sts onto stitch holder for neckband, work in patt to end.
Complete to match first side, reversing shapings.

BANDED STRIPE crewneck sweater

SLEEVES

Using 3¼mm (no 10/US 3) needles, cast on 56 sts with yarn D.

Work rib

Work rib as given for Back and AT THE SAME TIME inc 1 st on last row. 57 sts.

Begin chart pattern

Change to 4mm (no 8/US 6) needles.

Using the intarsia technique described in the basic information (see page 10), joining in and breaking off colours as required, reading odd numbered K rows from right to left and even numbered P rows from left to right, beg with a K row, work in patt from sleeve chart, which is worked entirely in st st, taking all inc sts into patt, inc 1 st at each end of 5th and then every foll 4th row until 109 sts.

Keeping chart correct, cont without shaping for 15 further rows.

Cast off (bind off) loosely and evenly.

FINISHING

Press all pieces on WS with a warm iron over a damp cloth. Join right shoulder seam using backstitch or mattress stitch.

Neckband

With RS facing, using 3¼mm (no 10/US 3) circular needle with yarn A, pick up and K 21 sts down Left Front neck, 22 sts across Front neck, 21 sts up Right Front neck and 40 sts across Back neck. 104 sts.

Work 24 rows in rib as given for Back. Change to yarn D.

Cast off (bind off) loosely and evenly in rib. Join left shoulder seam using backstitch or mattress stitch. Sew in sleeves using backstitch or mattress stitch, matching centre of sleeves to shoulder seam. Join side seams and sleeve seams using backstitch or mattress stitch. See the basic information (page 13) for further finishing instructions.

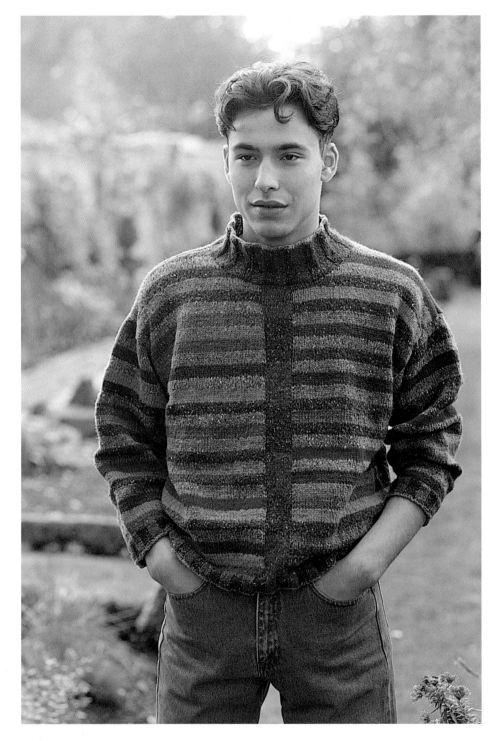

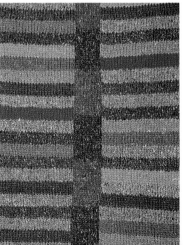

Key

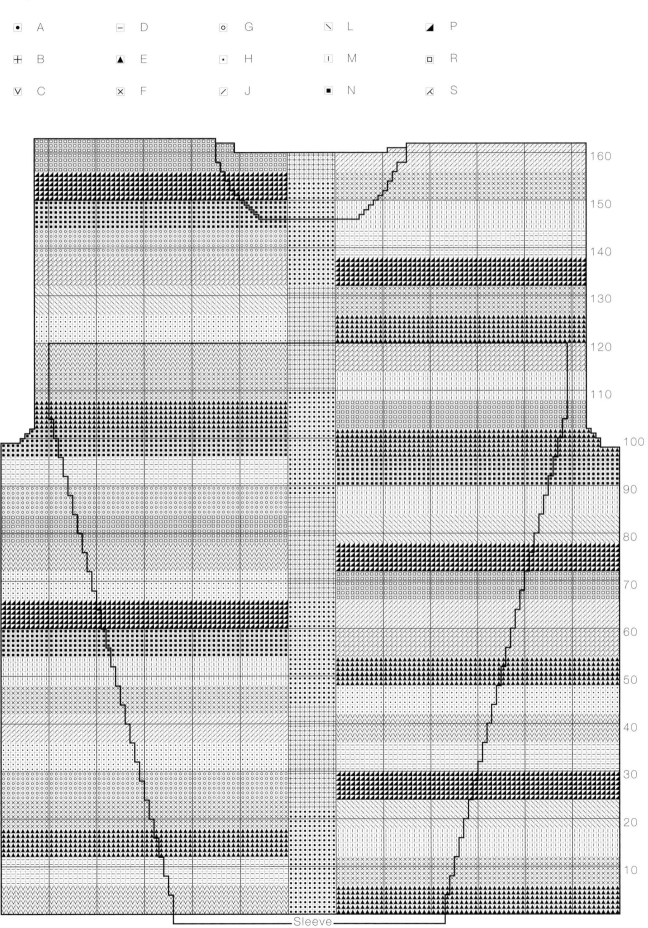

Sleeve

PRISONER crewneck sweater

Cartoon-like prisoner costumes with black arrows on white suits featured in the old movies have always grabbed me as being an amusing and intriguingly bold image. I've also always been struck by the bold use of arrows on road signs. When I repeated the strong arrow motif on this sweater I felt a close connection with the Pop artists who take pedestrian images and make them into art. Staggering the arrows on a smouldering ground of reds with rhythmic stripes gives a sense of movement to this design.

Yarn

Rowan Felted Tweed and Rowan DK Tweed

One size to fit a range of sizes
To fit up to chest   122cm (48 in)

A	Rowan Felted Tweed	dark brown (145)	1 x 50g
B	Rowan Felted Tweed	russett red (144)	7 x 50g
C	Rowan DK Tweed	dark red (868)	2 x 50g
D	Rowan DK Tweed	green (866)	1 x 50g
E	Rowan DK Tweed	mid-blue (862)	1 x 50g
F	Rowan Felted Tweed	black (135)	1 x 50g
G	Rowan Felted Tweed	navy blue (133)	1 x 50g
H	Rowan Felted Tweed	purple-pink (139)	1 x 50g

Needles

1 pair 3¼mm (no 10/US 3) needles
1 pair 4mm (no 8/US 6) needles
stitch holder

Tension

22 stitches and 32 rows to 10cm (4 in)
measured over patterned stocking
(stockinette) stitch using 4mm (no 8/US 6)
needles.

BACK

Using 3¼mm (no 10/US 3) needles, cast on
132 sts with yarn A.

Work rib

Work 6 rows in K2, P2 rib.
Change to yarn B.
Cont in rib as set until work measures 6cm
(2⅓ in), thus ending with a WS row.

Begin chart pattern

Change to 4mm (no 8/US 6) needles.
Using the intarsia technique described in the
basic information (see page 10), joining in
and breaking off colours as required, reading
odd numbered K rows from right to left and
even numbered P rows from left to right, beg
with a K row, work in patt from Back chart,
which is worked entirely in st st, until chart
row 194 has been completed, but AT THE
SAME TIME foll stripe sequence for
background as folls:
Work 2 rows in st st with yarn A.
Work 12 rows in st st with yarn B.
Work 2 rows in st st with yarn A.
Work 2 rows in st st with yarn C.
Work 2 rows in st st with yarn B.
Work 2 rows in st st with yarn C.
Work 4 rows in st st with yarn B.
Work 2 rows in st st with yarn A.
Work 8 rows in st st with yarn B.
Work 4 rows in st st with yarn C.
Rep stripe sequence throughout chart.

Shape back neck

Divide for neck shaping on next row as folls:
Next row (RS): Work in patt until 50 sts on
right-hand needle, turn, leaving rem sts on
stitch holder.
Work each side of neck separately.
Next row: Keeping chart correct, cast off
(bind off) 4 sts, work in patt to end.
Cast off (bind off) rem 46 sts.
With RS facing, rejoin yarn to rem sts on
stitch holder, cast off (bind off) centre 32 sts,
work in patt to end.
Complete to match first side, reversing
shapings.

FRONT

Work as given for Back until chart row 180 has
been completed, thus ending with a WS row.

Shape neck

Divde for neck shaping on next row as folls:
Next row (RS): Work in patt until 59 sts on
right-hand needle, turn, leaving rem sts on
stitch holder.
Work each side of neck separately.
Next row: Keeping chart correct, cast off
(bind off) 2 sts at neck edge on next and foll
alt (other) row.
Dec 1 st at neck edge on every foll row until
46 sts rem.
Cont without shaping until Front has same
number of rows as Back to shoulder, thus

ending with a WS row.
Cast off (bind off) rem 46 sts.
With RS facing, rejoin yarn to rem sts on
stitch holder, cast off (bind off) centre 14 sts,
work in patt to end.
Complete to match first side, reversing
shapings.

SLEEVES (MAKE TWO)

Using 3¼mm (no 10/US 3) needles, cast on
48 sts with yarn A.

Work rib

Work rib as given for Back.

Begin chart pattern

Change to 4mm (no 8/US 6) needles.
Using the intarsia technique described in the
basic information (see page 10), joining in
and breaking off colours as required, work 14
rows in stripe sequence as given for Back.
Cont in stripe sequence but AT THE SAME
TIME using chart for reference place three
arrows up the centre of each Sleeve, one on
top of the other, the first worked in yarn E, the
second worked in yarn F, and the third
worked in yarn H for Left Sleeve and the first
worked in yarn H, the second worked in yarn
D, and the third worked in yarn G for Right
Sleeve, taking all inc sts into patt, inc 1 st at
each end of every 4th row until 116 sts.
Cont without shaping until final arrow motif
has been completed.

Cont without shaping for 1 further row.
Cast off (bind off) loosely and evenly.

FINISHING
Press all pieces on WS with a warm iron over a damp cloth. Join right shoulder seam using backstitch or mattress stitch.

Neckband
With RS facing, using 3¼mm (no 10/US 3) needles with yarn B, pick up and K 100 sts evenly around neck.

Work 7 rows in rib as given for Back.
Change to yarn A.
Work 4 further rows in rib.
Cast off (bind off) loosely and evenly in rib.
Join left shoulder seam usng backstitch or mattress stitch. Sew in sleeves using backstitch or mattress stitch, matching centre of sleeves to shoulder seam. Join side and sleeve seams using backstitch or mattress stitch. See the basic information (page 13) for further finishing instructions.

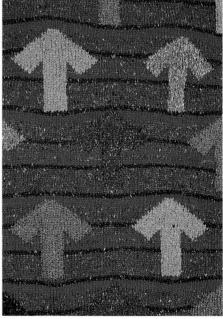

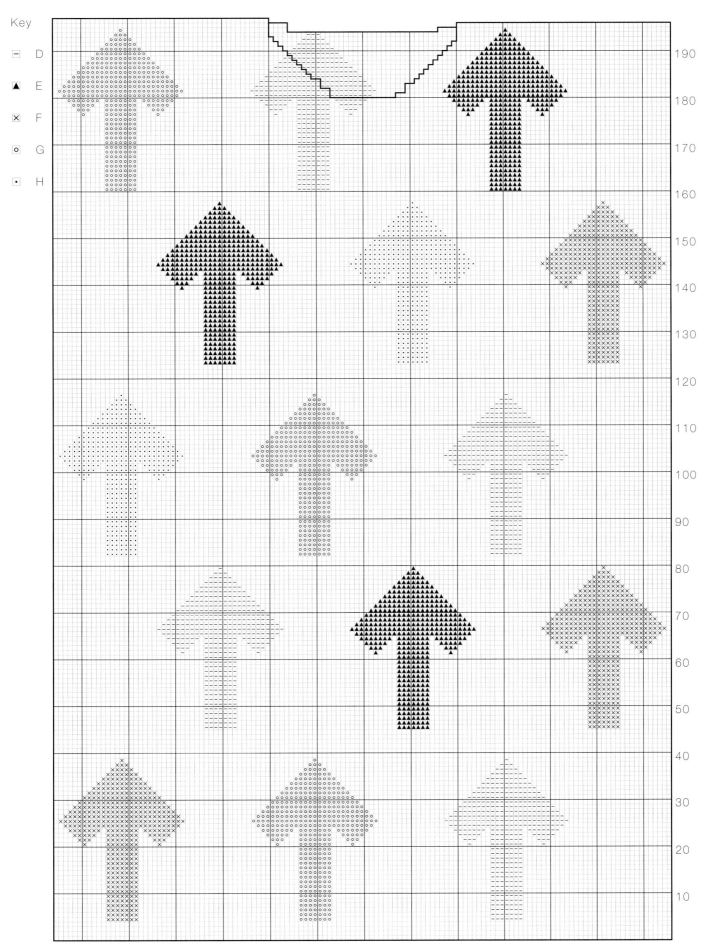

SHARK crewneck sweater

This design shows my minimal, purist side. Rather than cramming many shades of colour into a pattern, working with just two colours to create an exciting design is a challenge I enjoy rising to meet. You might be forgiven for thinking it was collaged strips of paper on a dark background that lead to this design, but it was, in fact, the ventilators on a sporty BMW, which reminded me of the gills on a shark, that inspired me. *Rowan Knitting Magazine* first featured this garment with dusty lavender waves on a charcoal black background, but my original colourway was this fiery, deep red on a rich, inky blue background.

Yarn
Rowan Wool Cotton

			Small	Medium	Large	Extra-large
To fit up to chest			97cm (38 in)	102cm (40 in)	107cm (42 in)	112cm (44 in)
A	Rowan Wool Cotton	navy blue (909)	15	15	16	16 x 50g
B	Rowan Wool Cotton	dark red (911)	1	1	1	1 x 50g

Needles
1 pair 3¼mm (no 10/US 3) needles
1 pair 4mm (no 8/US 6) needles
stitch holder

Tension
22 stitches and 30 rows to 10cm (4 in) measured over patterned stocking (stockinette) stitch using 4mm (no 8/US 6) needles.

BACK
Using 3¼mm (no 10/US 3) needles, cast on 139 (145: 151: 157) sts with yarn A.
Work rib
Row 1 (RS): P2, * K3, P3, rep from * to last 5 sts, K3, P2.
Row 2: K2, * P3, K3, rep from * to last 5 sts, P3, K2.
Work 14 further rows in rib as set, thus ending with a WS row.
Change to 4mm (no 8/US 6) needles.
Beg with a K row, cont in st st until Back measures 40 (41: 41: 42) cm or 15¾ (16¼: 16¼: 16½) in, thus ending with a WS row.
Shape armholes
Cast off (bind off) 4 sts at beg of next 2 rows. 131 (137: 143: 149) sts.
Dec 1 st at each end of next 7 rows. 117 (123: 129: 135) sts.
Cont without shaping until armhole measures 28 (28: 29: 29) cm or 11 (11: 11½: 11½) in, thus ending with a WS row.
Shape shoulders and back neck
Cast off (bind off) 12 (13: 14: 15) sts at beg of next 2 rows. 93 (97: 101: 105) sts.
Divide for neck shaping on next row as folls:
Next row (RS): Cast off (bind off) 12 (13: 14: 15) sts, K until 16 (17: 18: 19) sts on right-hand needle, turn, leaving rem sts on stitch holder.
Work each side of neck separately.

Next row: Cast off (bind off) 4 sts, P to end.
Cast off (bind off) rem 12 (13: 14: 15) sts.
With RS facing, rejoin yarn to rem sts on stitch holder, cast off (bind off) centre 37 sts for neckband, K to end.
Complete to match first side, reversing shapings.

FRONT
Work as given for Back until Front measures 22cm (8½ in) from cast-on edge, thus ending with a WS row.
Begin chart pattern
Join in yarn B, using the intarsia technique as described in the basic information (see page 10), joining in and breaking off yarns as required, reading odd numbered K rows from right to left and even numbered P rows from left to right, working entirely in st st, place chart as folls:
Next row (RS): K16 (19: 22: 25), work 107 sts from chart across chart row 1, K16 (19: 22: 25).
Next row: P16 (19: 22: 25), work 107 sts from chart across chart row 2, P16 (19: 22: 25).
Cont working from chart as set until chart row 98 has been completed, thus ending with a WS row.
Cont in st st using yarn A only and AT THE SAME TIME work as given for Back until 22 rows less have been worked than for Back to

start of shoulder shaping, thus ending with a WS row.
Shape front neck
Divide for neck shaping on next row as folls:
Next row (RS): K50 (53: 56: 59), turn, leaving rem sts on stitch holder.
Work each side of neck separately.
Next row: Cast off (bind off) 4 sts, P to end. 46 (49: 52: 55) sts.
Dec 1 st at neck edge on next 5 rows, then on foll 4 alt (other) rows, then on foll 4th row. 36 (39: 42: 45) sts.
Cont without shaping for 3 further rows, thus ending with a WS row.
Shape shoulder
Cast off (bind off) 12 (13: 14: 15) sts at beg of next and foll alt (other) row. 12 (13: 14: 15) sts.
Work 1 row.
Cast off (bind off) rem 12 (13: 14: 15) sts.
With RS facing, rejoin yarn to rem sts on stitch holder, cast off (bind off) centre 17 sts for neckband, K to end.
Complete to match first side, reversing shapings.

SLEEVES (MAKE TWO)
Using 3¼mm (no 10/US 3) needles, cast on 67 (67: 69: 69) sts with yarn A.
Work rib
Row 1 (RS): K2 (2: 3: 3), P3, * K3, P3, rep

Key ☐ A ● B

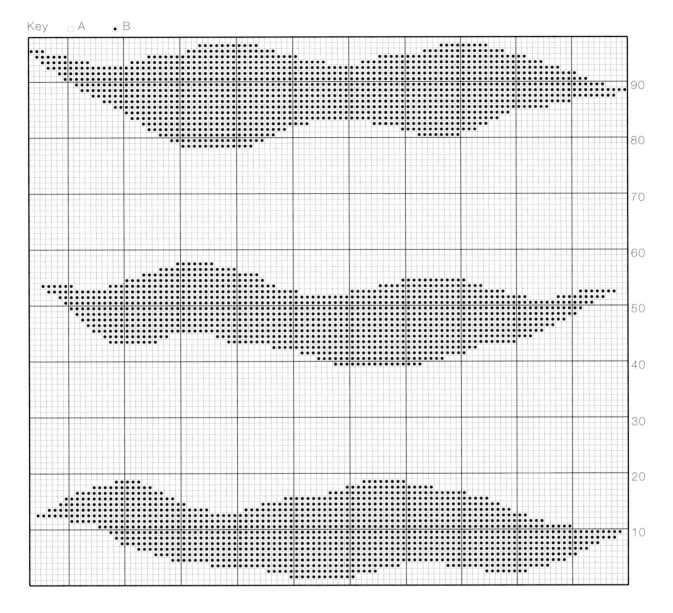

from * to last 2 (2: 3: 3) sts, K2 (2: 3: 3).
Row 2: P2 (2: 3: 3), K3, * P3, K3, rep from *
to last 2 (2: 3: 3) sts, P2 (2: 3: 3).
Work 14 further rows in rib as set, thus
ending with a WS row.
Change to 4mm (no 8/US 6) needles.
Beg with a K row, cont in st st, inc 1 st at
each end of 3rd and every foll 6th row until
73 (73: 75: 75) sts, then on every foll 4th row
until 123 (123: 127: 127) sts.
Cont without shaping until Sleeve measures
49 (49: 50: 50) cm or 19¼ (19¼: 19½:
19½) in from cast-on edge, thus ending with
a WS row.

Shape top
Cast off (bind off) 4 sts at beg of next 2 rows.
115 (115: 119: 119) sts.
Dec 1 st at each end on next and foll 4 alt
(other) rows. 105 (105: 109: 109) sts.

Cont without shaping for 1 further row.
Cast off (bind off) rem 105 (105: 109:
109) sts.

FINISHING
Press all pieces on WS with a warm iron
over a damp cloth. Join right shoulder
seam using backstitch or mattress stitch.
Crew-neck version only
Neckband
With RS facing, using 3¼mm (no 10/
US 3) needles with yarn A, pick up and K
29 sts down Left Front neck, 17 sts
across Front neck, 29 sts up Right Front
neck and 45 sts across Back neck.
120 sts.
Row 1 (WS): * K3, P3, rep from * to end.
Rep last row until neckband measures
5cm (2 in).

High-neck version only
Neckband
With RS facing, using 4mm needles (no
8/US 6) with yarn A, pick up and K 29 sts
down Left Front neck, 17 sts across Front
neck, 29 sts up Right Front neck and 45
sts across Back neck. 120 sts.
Row 1 (WS): * K3, P3, rep from * to end.
Rep last row until neckband measures
10cm (4 in).
Both versions
Cast off (bind off) loosely and evenly in rib.
Join left shoulder seam using backstitch or
mattress stitch. Sew in sleeves using
backstitch or mattress stitch, matching centre
of sleeves to shoulder seam. Join side seams
and sleeve seams using backstitch or
mattress stitch. See the basic information
(page 13) for further finishing instructions.

KUBRA v-neck waistcoat

African appliqué and patchwork get my attention every time because their design, rhythm and primitive sensibilities sing a refreshing song. It is as if there is a passage of mythical stories or messages entwined in the graphic markings. I'm fortunate to have access to a small library of ethnic textiles books, which informed this design. Any good book shop or your local library will have a selection of books on ethnic art and textiles, which will be oozing with good design ideas. I originally designed a version of African appliqué in 4-ply yarns for the Rowan Collection. Here I have done an upscale version using Rowan Felted Tweed and Rowan DK Tweed: it is much faster to knit. Wasn't I lucky to find this distressed wall for this waistcoat to be photographed against?

Yarn
Rowan Felted Tweed and Rowan DK Tweed

One size to fit a range of sizes
To fit up to chest   117cm (46 in)

A	Rowan Felted Tweed	green-blue (131)	3 x 50g
B	Rowan DK Tweed	green (866)	1 x 50g
C	Rowan Felted Tweed	navy blue (133)	2 x 50g
D	Rowan Felted Tweed	blue-grey (141)	1 x 50g
E	Rowan Felted Tweed	green-gold (138)	2 x 50g
F	Rowan Felted Tweed	rose pink (137)	2 x 50g
G	Rowan DK Tweed	oatmeal (850)	1 x 50g
H	Rowan Felted Tweed	pale gold (136)	1 x 50g
J	Rowan DK Tweed	yellow-green (863)	2 x 50g
L	Rowan DK Tweed	pale grey-green (851)	1 x 50g

Needles
1 pair 3¼mm (no 10/US 3) needles
1 pair 4mm (no 8/US 6) needles
1 3¼mm (no 10/US 3) circular needle
stitch holder

Buttons
7

Tension
21 stitches and 27 rows to 10cm (4 in) measured over patterned stocking (stockinette) stitch using 4mm (no 8/US 6) needles.

BACK
Using 3¼mm (no 10/US 3) needles, cast on 112 sts with yarn A.

Work hem
Beg with a K row, work 6 rows in st st, thus ending with a WS row.
P 2 rows to form hemline ridge, thus ending with a WS row.

Begin chart pattern
Change to 4mm (no 8/US 6) needles.
Using the Fair Isle technique described in the basic information (see page 11), knitting in yarns as required, reading odd numbered K rows from right to left and even numbered P rows from left to right, beg with a K row, work in patt from Back chart, which is worked entirely in st st, taking all inc sts into patt, inc 1 st where marked on chart until chart row 100 has been completed, but AT THE SAME TIME foll stripe sequence for background as folls:
Work 8 rows in st st with yarn A.
Work 2 rows in st st with yarn E.
Work 2 rows in st st with yarn D.
Work 12 rows in st st with yarn A.
Work 2 rows in st st with yarn D.
Work 6 rows in st st with yarn A.
Work 1 row in st st with yarn C.

Work 2 rows in st st with yarn D.
Work 1 row in st st with yarn B.
Work 6 rows in st st with yarn A.
Work 2 rows in st st with yarn D.
Work 2 rows in st st with yarn C.
Work 26 rows in st st with yarn A.
Work 1 row in st st with yarn E.
Work 2 rows in st st with yarn B.
Work 16 rows in st st with yarn A.
Work 1 row in st st with yarn C.
Work 2 rows in st st with yarn D.
Work 1 row in st st with yarn B.
Work 16 rows in st st with yarn A.
Work 2 rows in st st with yarn D.
Work 2 rows in st st with yarn C.
Work 13 rows in st st with yarn A.
Work 2 rows in st st with yarn C.
Rep stripe sequence throughout chart.

Shape armholes
Keeping chart correct, cast off (bind off) 5 sts at beg of next 2 rows and 3 sts at beg of foll 2 rows. 104 sts.
Dec 1 st at each end of next 12 rows. 80 sts.
Cont without shaping until chart row 168 has been completed, thus ending with a WS row.

Shape back neck
Divide for neck shaping on next row as folls:

Next row (RS): Keeping chart correct, work in patt until 23 sts on right-hand needle, turn, leaving rem sts on stitch holder.
Work each side of neck separately.
Cont without shaping for 1 further row.
Cast off (bind off) rem 23 sts.
With RS facing, rejoin yarn to rem sts on stitch holder, cast off (bind off) centre 34 sts for neckband, work in patt to end.
Complete to match first side, reversing shapings.

LEFT FRONT
Using 3¼mm (no 10/US 3) needles, cast on 56 sts with yarn A.

Work hem
Work hem as given for Back.

Begin chart pattern
Change to 4mm (no 8/US 6) needles.
Using the Fair Isle technique described in the basic information (see page 11), knitting in yarns as required, reading odd numbered K rows rom right to left and even numbered P rows from left to right, beg with a K row, work in patt from Left Front chart, which is worked entirely in st st, taking all inc sts into patt, inc 1 st where marked on chart until chart row

100 has been completed, but AT THE SAME TIME time foll stripe sequence for background as given for Back.

Shape armhole and neck

Next row (RS): Keeping chart correct, cast off (bind off) 5 sts, work in patt to end. 55 sts.
Cont without shaping for 1 further row.

Next row (RS): Cast off (bind off) 3 sts, work in patt to end. 52 sts.
Cont without shaping for 1 further row.
Dec 1 st at armhole edge on next 12 rows and AT THE SAME TIME dec 1 st at neck edge on 5th and every foll 4th row until 24 sts rem.
Dec 1 st on foll alt (other) row. 23 sts.
Cont without shaping until Left Front has same number of rows as Back to shoulder, thus ending with a WS row.
Cast off (bind off).

RIGHT FRONT

Work as given for Left Front, but foll chart for Right Front, reversing all shapings.

FINISHING

Press all pieces on WS with a warm iron over a damp cloth. Join both shoulder seams using backstitch or mattress stitch.

Neck and front bands (worked in one piece)

With RS facing, using 3¼mm (no 10/US 3) circular needle with yarn A, pick up and K 82 sts up Right Front from hemline to beg of neck shaping, 50 sts up Right Front neck, 36 sts across Back neck, 50 sts down Left Front neck, and 82 sts down Left Front from beg of neck shaping to hemline. 300 sts.
Using the Fair Isle technique as described in the basic information (see page 11), working in st st as folls:

Row 1: * K4 with yarn A, K4 with yarn C, rep from * to 4 sts, K 4 with yarn A.

Row 2: * P4 with yarn A, P4 with yarn C, rep from * to 4 sts, P4 with yarn A.
Rep last 2 rows once more.

Make buttonholes

1st buttonhole row: Work in patt as set until 222 sts on right-hand needle, * cast off (bind off) 2 sts knitwise, work in patt as set until 10 sts on right-hand needle after last cast-off (bind-off), rep from * 5 times, cast off (bind off) 2 sts knitwise, work in patt to end.

2nd buttonhole row: Cont in patt as set, casting on 2 sts over those cast off (bound off) on previous row.
Cont in patt as set for a further 2 rows.
Change to yarn A only.
P 1 row.
Cont in st st for a further 3 rows.
Work 1st and 2nd buttonhole rows once more.
Cont in st st for a further 3 rows.
Cast off (bind off).

Armhole bands

With RS facing, using 3¼mm (no 10/US 3) needles with yarn A, pick up and K 128 sts evenly around armhole edge.

Next row (WS): * K2 with yarn A, P2 with yarn B, rep from * to end.

Next row (RS): * K2 with yarn B, P2 with yarn A, rep from * to end.
Cont in patt as set for 1 further row.
Keeping patt as set, cast off (bind off) loosely and evenly in rib.
Join side seams using backstitch or mattress stitch. Fold bottom hem onto WS along hemline ridge and slip-stitch into position. Oversew double buttonholes. Sew buttons on to correspond with buttonholes. See the basic information (page 13) for further finishing instructions.

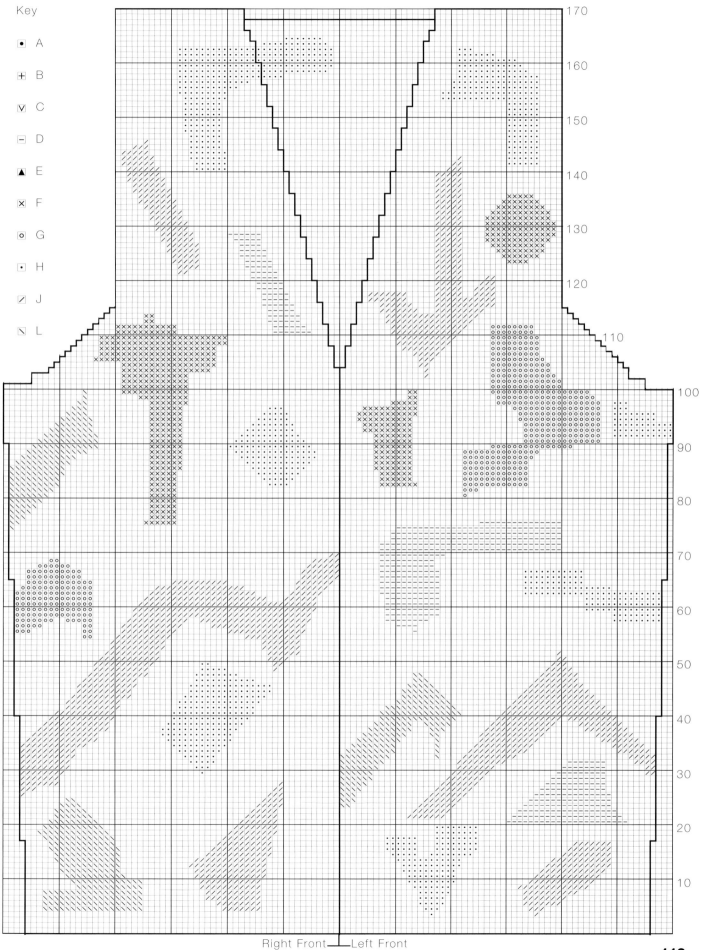

KUBRA v-neck waistcoat

Key

• A

+ B

∨ C

− D

▲ E

✕ F

◉ G

• H

⧄ J

⧅ L

Right Front ⊥ Left Front

SHELVES crewneck sweater

This sweater is a play on the repetition of wide rectangles, which look like multi-coloured filing boxes or books standing on shelves. While the colours of the rectangles are quite cool and strong, the silver grey horizontal bands help to lift the palette. I had originally thought of this design for a woman's sweater but when I slipped it onto a guy, I was amazed at how good it looks on both sexes. Knitted in the soft Jaeger Matchmaker Merino 4 ply and Rowan True 4 ply Botany yarns, it is finished with a vertical striped band for bottom edge, the cuffs and high neck.

Yarn

Jaeger Matchmaker Merino 4 ply and Rowan True 4 ply Botany

One size to fit a range of sizes
To fit up to chest   122cm (48 in)

A	Jaeger Matchmaker Merino 4 ply	mid-grey (639)	7 x 50g
B	Rowan True 4 ply Botany	mid-navy blue (548)	2 x 50g
C	Jaeger Matchmaker Merino 4 ply	camel (718)	1 x 50g
D	Jaeger Matchmaker Merino 4 ply	heather (701)	1 x 50g
E	Jaeger Matchmaker Merino 4 ply	bottle green (814)	1 x 50g
F	Jaeger Matchmaker Merino 4 ply	brown-burgundy (704)	1 x 50g
G	Jaeger Matchmaker Merino 4 ply	mid-blue (740)	1 x 50g
H	Rowan True 4 ply Botany	purple (557)	1 x 25g
J	Rowan True 4 ply Botany	navy blue (563)	1 x 50g
L	Rowan True 4 ply Botany	pale blue-green (552)	1 x 50g

All yarns are to be worked double.

Needles

1 pair 3¼mm (no 10/US 3) needles
1 pair 4mm (no 8/US 6) needles
stitch holder

Tension

22 stitches and 29 rows to 10cm (4 in) measured over patterned stocking (stockinette) stitch using 4mm (no 8/US 6) needles.

Pattern tip

When working this pattern, use the Fair Isle technique (see page 11) for ribbings. For main part of body use the Intarsia method by using separate bobbins or length for each colour.

BACK

Using 3¼mm (no 10/US 3) needles, cast on 132 sts with yarn B.
Work in K2, P2 rib as folls:
Row 1: * K2 with yarn B, P2 with yarn A, rep from * to end.
Row 2: * K2 with yarn A, P2 with yarn B, rep from * to end.
Rep last 2 rows until rib measures 6cm (2¼ in) ending with a WS row.
Begin chart pattern
Change to 4mm (no 8/US 6) needles.
Using the intarsia technique described in the basic information (see page 10), joining in and breaking off colours as required, reading odd numbered K rows from right to left and even numbered P rows from left to right, beg with a K row, work in patt from body chart, which is worked entirely in st st, until chart row 194 has been worked, thus ending with a WS row.
Shape back neck
Divide for neck shaping on next row as folls:
Next row (RS): Work in patt until 47 sts on right-hand needle, turn, leaving rem sts on stitch holder.
Work each side of neck separately.

Cont without shaping for 1 further row.
Cast off (bind off) rem 47 sts.
With RS facing, rejoin yarn to rem sts on stitch holder, cast off (bind off) centre 38 sts, work in patt to end.
Complete to match first side, reversing shapings.

FRONT

Work as given for Back until chart row 174 has been worked, thus ending with a WS row.
Shape neck
Divde for neck shaping on next row as folls:
Next row (RS): Work in patt until 57 sts on right-hand needle, turn, leaving rem sts on stitch holder.
Work each side of neck separately.
Next row: Cast off (bind off) 2 sts at neck edge, work in patt to end.
Cont to dec 1 st at neck edge on next 5 rows, then on foll 3 alt (other) rows. 47 sts.
Cont without shaping until Front has same number of rows as Back to shoulder.
Cast off (bind off) rem 47 sts.
With RS facing, rejoin yarn to rem sts on stitch holder, cast off (bind off) centre 18 sts,

work in patt to end.
Complete to match first side, reversing shapings.

SLEEVES

Using 3¼mm (no 10/US 3) needles, cast on 76 sts with yarn B
Work in rib as given for Back.
Begin chart pattern
Change to 4mm (no 6/US 6) needles.
Using the intarsia technique described in the basic information (see page 10), joining in and breaking off colours as required, reading odd numbered K rows from right to left and even numbered P rows from left to right, beg with a K row, work in patt from sleeve chart, which is worked entirely in st st, taking all inc sts into patt, inc 1 st at each end of every 6th row 15 times, then every 5th row 4 times. 114 sts.
Cont without shaping for 10 further rows or until sleeve measures 48cm (18¾ in).
Cast off (bind off).

FINISHING

Press all pieces on WS with a warm iron over a damp cloth. Join right shoulder seam using backstitch or mattress stitch.

Neckband

With RS facing, using 3¼mm (no 10/US 3) needles with yarn A, pick up and K 100 sts evenly around neck.

Work 7cm (2¾ in) in rib as for given for Back. Change to yarn A only.

Cast off (bind off) loosely and evenly in rib. Join left shoulder seam using backstitch or mattress stitch. Sew in sleeves using backstitch or mattress stitch, matching centre of sleeves to shoulder seam. Join side seams and sleeve seams using backstitch or mattress stitch. See the basic information (page 13) for further finishing instructions.

Key

- ⊡ A
- ⊞ B
- ⊽ C
- ⊟ D
- ▲ E
- ⊠ F
- ⊙ G
- ⊡ H
- ◩ J
- ◪ L

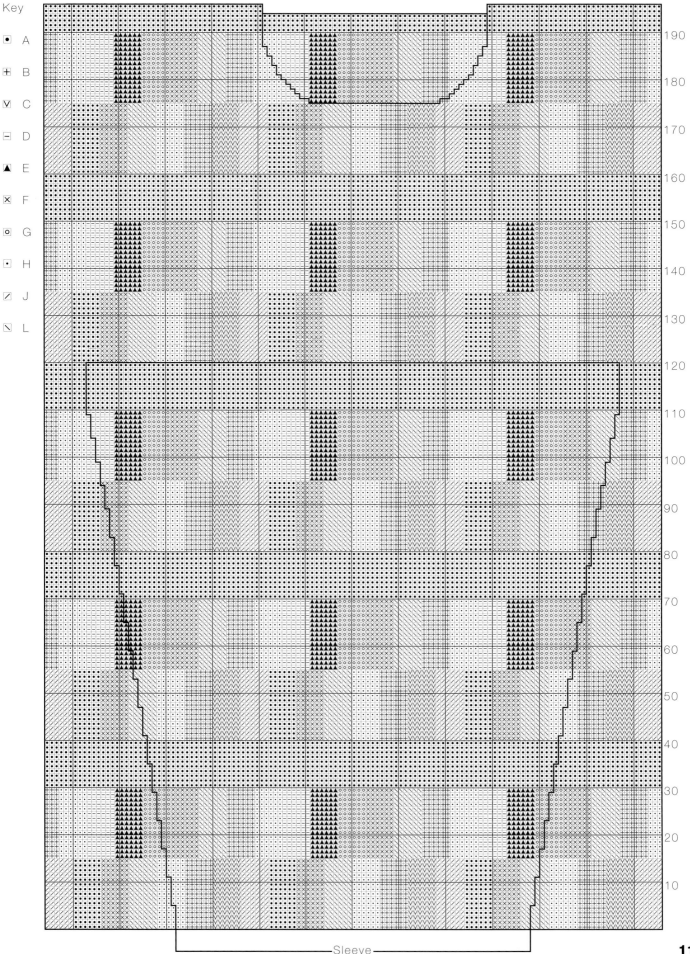

Sleeve

117

AURORA slipover

Like so many good ideas, the inspiration for Aurora came to me while I was flipping through a book on kilim carpets. The original design had a very set repeat for the motif, which I wanted to avoid. The result is this waistcoat where the different shades of tweed yarn in the background and motifs remind me of the mysterious night sky. Using blue, green and cranberry tweed yarns for the background, with oatmeal and dusty pink highlights, the waistcoat knits up beautifully as a simple Fair Isle pattern. I've chosen a handsome dark palette for this garment, but a design like this can be easily re-coloured. For instance, consider shades of warm browns and deep blue with tones of steely grey for the motifs – or you might have your own inspiration to play with.

Yarn

Rowan DK Tweed and Rowan Felted Tweed

One size to fit a range of sizes
To fit up to chest   102cm (40 in)

A	Rowan DK Tweed	dusky pink (861)	1 x 50g
B	Rowan Felted Tweed	rose pink (137)	2 x 50g
C	Rowan Felted Tweed	green-gold (138)	2 x 50g
D	Rowan Felted Tweed	forest green (130)	1 x 50g
E	Rowan Felted Tweed	burgundy (134)	2 x 50g
F	Rowan Felted Tweed	navy blue (133)	2 x 50g

Needles

1 pair 3mm (no 11/US 2) needles
1 pair 3¾mm (no 9/US 5) needles
stitch holder

Tension

23 stitches and 27 rows to 10cm (4 in) measured over patterned stocking (stockinette) stitch using 3¾mm (no 9/US 5) needles.

BACK

Using 3mm (no 11/US 2) needles, cast on 126 sts with yarn F.

Work rib

Work 24 rows in K1, P1 rib in stripe sequence as folls:
Work 3 rows with yarn F.
Work 2 rows with yarn A.
Work 3 rows with yarn E.
Work 2 rows with yarn C.
Work 3 rows with yarn D.
Work 1 row with yarn B.
Work 3 rows with yarn F.
Work 2 rows with yarn D.
Work 3 rows with yarn E.
Work 2 rows with yarn C.

Begin chart pattern

Change to 3¾mm (no 9/US 5) needles.
Using the Fair Isle technique described in the basic information (see page 11), knitting in yarns as required, reading odd numbered K rows from right to left and even numbered P rows from left to right, beg with a K row, work 32 row patt rep from body chart, which is worked entirely in st st, until work measures 40cm, thus ending with a WS row.

Shape armholes

Keeping chart correct, cast off (bind off) 10 sts at beg of next 2 rows and 2 sts at beg of foll 4 rows. 92 sts.
Dec 1 st at each end of next 3 rows. 89 sts.

Cont without shaping until work measures 63cm (24¾ in), thus ending with a WS row.

Shape back neck

Divide for neck shaping on next row as folls:
Next row (RS): Work in patt until 25 sts on right-hand needle, turn, leaving rem sts on stitch holder.
Work each side of neck separately.
Cont without shaping for 1 further row.
Cast off (bind off) rem 25 sts.
With RS facing, rejoin yarn to rem sts on stitch holder, slip centre 42 sts on to stitch holder for neckband, work in patt to end.
Complete to match first side, reversing shapings.

FRONT

Work as given for Back, working armhole shaping until 98 sts rem.

Shape armholes and neck

Divide for neck shaping on next rows as folls:
Next row (RS): Work 2 tog, work in patt until 48 sts on right-hand needle, turn, leaving rem sts on stitch holder.
Work each side of neck separately.
Keeping chart correct, dec 1 st at neck edge on every foll alt (other) 2nd and 3rd rows until 25 sts rem and AT THE SAME TIME work the armhole shapings as given for Back.
Cont without shaping until Front has same number of rows as Back to shoulder, thus

ending with a WS row.
Cast off (bind off).
With RS facing, rejoin yarn to rem sts, work in patt to end.
Complete to match first side, reversing all shapings.

FINISHING

Press all pieces on WS with a warm iron over a damp cloth. Join right shoulder seams using backstitch or mattress stitch.

Neckband

With RS facing, using 3mm (no 11/US 2) needles with yarn F, pick up and K 58 sts down Left Front neck, 1 st for centre of v-neck (mark this stitch), 58 sts up Right Front neck, and 42 sts across Back neck. 159 sts.
Row 1: Using yarn F, work in rib to 2 sts before marked st, P2tog tbl, P1, P2tog, work in rib to end.
Row 2: Using yarn F, work in rib to 2 sts before marked st, K2tog tbl, K1, K2tog, work in rib to end.
Cont in the stripe sequence as folls and AT THE SAME TIME cont to dec as set:
Work 1 row with yarn F.
Work 2 rows with yarn D.
Work 2 rows with yarn E.
Work 1 row with yarn C.
Cast off (bind off) loosely and evenly in rib with yarn D.

Armhole bands

Join left shoulder seam using backstitch or
mattress stitch.

With RS facing, using 3mm (no 11/US 2)
needles with yarn F, pick up and K 130 sts
evenly around armhole edge.

Work 8 rows in K1, P1 rib foll stripe sequence
as given for neckband.

Cast off (bind off) loosely and evenly in rib
with yarn D.

Join side seams using backstitch or mattress
stitch. See the basic information (page 13) for
further finishing instructions.

Key

- •   A
- +   B
- V   C
- –   D
- ▲   E
- ×   F

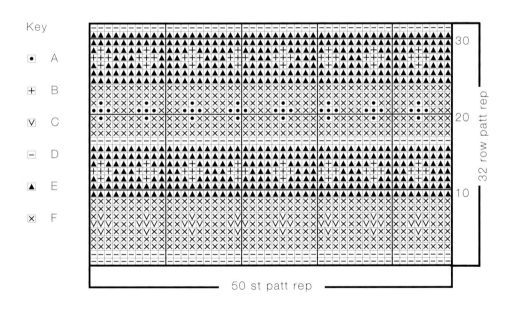

50 st patt rep

32 row patt rep

MARRAKECH crewneck sweater

This sweater simulates a loose tangle of dark metal lattice, with rich globes of jewel-coloured glass rock caught in the weave. There is a wonderful sense of mystery about this design – like looking through Moroccan trelliswork at a mirage in the desert beyond. As a child, I can recall peeping through a neighbour's lattice fence at some tempting apple trees on the way to school, which gave the same illusion. Another lattice structure that sticks in my mind is the gates to the Guggenheim museum in Venice. Even though the museum was closed when I visited, I came away with the stimulating design idea used in this garment.

Yarn

Rowan True 4 ply Botany and Jaeger Matchmaker Merino DK

One size to fit a range of sizes
To fit up to chest 107cm (42 in)

A	Rowan True 4 ply Botany	black (546)	4 x 50g
B	Jaeger Matchmaker Merino 4 ply	olive green (723)	1 x 50g
C	Rowan True 4 ply Botany	purple (581)	1 x 50g
D	Rowan True 4 ply Botany	burgundy (547)	1 x 50g
E	Rowan True 4 ply Botany	dark red (549)	1 x 50g
F	Rowan True 4 ply Botany	silver-grey (782)	1 x 50g
G	Rowan True 4 ply Botany	blue-green (552)	1 x 50g
H	Rowan True 4 ply Botany	navy blue (563)	1 x 50g
J	Rowan True 4 ply Botany	mid-navy blue (574)	1 x 50g
L	Jaeger Matchmaker Merino 4 ply	turquoise (569)	1 x 50g

Needles

1 pair 3mm (no 11/US 2) needles
1 pair 3¼mm (no 10/US 3) needles
stitch holder

Tension

29 stitches and 32 rows to 10cm (4 in) measured over patterned stocking (stockinette) stitch using 3¼mm (no 10/US 3) needles.

BACK

Using 3mm (no 11/US 2) needles, cast on 156 sts with yarn B.

Work rib

Work 1 row in K1, P1 rib.
Change to yarn A.
Cont in as set until Back measures 6cm (2¼ in), thus ending with a WS row.

Begin chart pattern

Change to 3¼mm (no 10/US 3) needles.
Using the intarsia technique described in the basic information (see page 10), joining in and breaking off colours as required, reading odd numbered K rows from right to left and even numbered P rows from left to right, beg with a K row, work in patt from 30 row patt rep body chart working the 2 row stripes within the diamonds in random colours, which is worked entirely in st st, until 190 rows have been completed, thus ending with a WS row.

Shape back neck

Divide for neck shaping on next row as folls:
Next row (RS): Work in patt until 64 sts on right-hand needle, turn, leaving rem sts on stitch holder.
Work each side of neck separately.

Next row: Keeping patt correct, cast off (bind off) 4 sts, work in patt to end. 60 sts.
Cast off (bind off) rem 60 sts.
With RS facing, rejoin yarn to rem sts on stitch holder, slip centre 28 sts on to stitch holder for neckband, work in patt to end.
Complete to match first side, reversing shapings.

FRONT

Work as given for Back until 168 rows of patt have been completed, thus ending with a WS row.

Shape front neck

Divide for neck shaping on next row as folls:
Next row (RS): Work in patt until 68 sts on right-hand needle, turn, leaving rem sts on stitch holder.
Work each side of neck separately.
Next row: Keeping patt correct, cast off (bind off) 4 sts, work in patt to end. 64 sts.
Dec 1 st at neck edge on every row until 60 sts rem.
Cont without shaping until Front has same number of rows as Back to shoulder, thus ending with a WS row.
Cast off (bind off) rem 60 sts.

With RS facing, rejoin yarn to rem sts, slip centre 20 sts onto stitch holder for neckband, work in patt to end.
Complete to match first side, reversing shapings.

SLEEVES (MAKE TWO)

Using 3mm (no 11/US 2) needles, cast on 68 sts with yarn B.

Work rib

Work rib as given for Back.

Begin chart pattern

Change to 3¼mm (no 10/US 3) needles.
Using the intarsia technique described in the basic information (see page 10), joining in and breaking off colours as required, reading odd numbered K rows from right to left and even numbered P rows from left to right, beg with a K row, work in patt from 30 row patt rep sleeve chart, working the 2 row stripes within the diamonds in random colours, which is worked entirely in st st, taking all inc sts into patt, inc 1 st at each end of 4th row and then every foll 4th row until 130 sts.
Keeping patt correct, cont without shaping until work measures 47cm (18½ in).
Cast off (bind off) loosely and evenly.

MARRAKECH crewneck sweater

Key

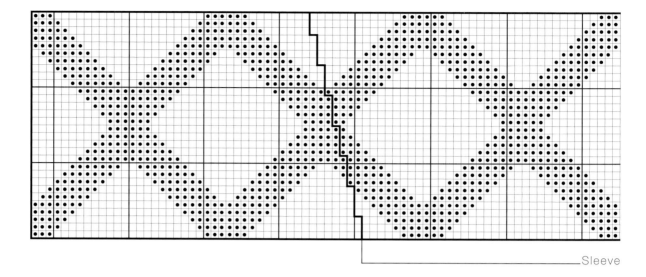

Sleeve

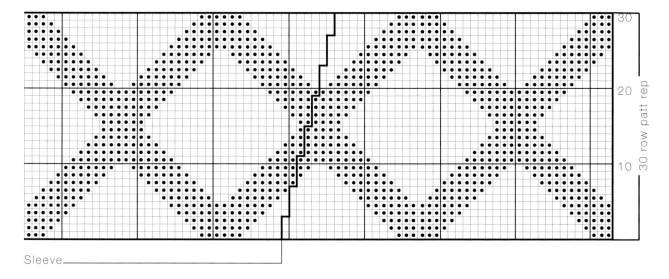

Sleeve

FINISHING

Press all pieces on WS with a warm iron over a damp cloth. Join right shoulder seam using backstitch or mattress stitch.

Neckband

With RS facing, using 3mm (no 11/US 2) needles with yarn A, pick up and K 28 sts down Left Front neck, 20 sts from stitch holder across Front neck, 28 sts up Right Front neck and 38 sts from stitch holder across Back neck. 114 sts.

Work 8 rows in K1, P1 rib.

Change to yarn B.

Work 1 row in rib as set.

Cast off (bind off) loosely and evenly in rib. Join left shoulder seam using backstitch or mattress stitch. Sew in sleeves using backstitch or mattress stitch, matching centre of sleeves to shoulder seam. Join side seams and sleeve seams using backstitch or mattress stitch. See the basic information (page 13) for further finishing instructions.

Yarn stockists and suppliers

Rowan Yarns and Jaeger Yarns addresses

Rowan and Jaeger yarns are widely available in yarn shops. For details of stockists and mail order sources of the yarns, please write to or contact the distributors listed on this page and the next page.
For Rowan yarns, you can also visit their website: www.rowanyarns.co.uk

Rowan Yarns

UNITED KINGDOM
HEAD OFFICE: Rowan Yarns, Green Lane Mill, Holmfirth, West Yorkshire HD7 1RW, England.
Tel: (01484) 681 881. Fax: (01484) 687 920.
Email: rowanmail@rowanyarns.co.uk

USA
DISTRIBUTOR: Rowan USA, 5 Northern Boulevard, Amherst, NH 03031.
Tel: (603) 886-5041/5043.
Email: wfibers@aol.com

AUSTRALIA
DISTRIBUTOR: Sunspun, 185 Canterbury Road, Canterbury, VIC 3126.
Tel: 03 9830 1609

BELGIUM
DISTRIBUTOR: Pavan, Koningin Astridlaan 78, B9000 Gent.
Tel: (09) 221 8594.

CANADA
DISTRIBUTORS:
Diamond Yarn, 9697 St Laurent, Montreal, Quebec H3L 2N1.
Tel: (514) 388-6188.
Diamond Yarn (Toronto), 155 Martin Ross, Unit 3, Toronto, Ontario M3J 2L9.
Tel (416) 736-6111.

DENMARK
STOCKISTS:
Aarhus: Ingers, Volden 19, 8000 Aarhus C.
Tel : 86 19 40 44.
Kobenhavn: Sommerfuglen: Vandkunsten 3, 1467 Kobenhavn K.
Tel : 33 32 82 90.
Email: mail@sommerfuglen.dk
Nykobing: Ruzicka, St Kirkestraede 5 B, 4800 Nykobing F.
Tel : 54 70 78 04. Email: anne-lise@rudzicka.dk
Roskilde: Garnhoekeren, Karen Olsdatterstraede 9, 4000 Roskilde.
Tel: 46 37 20 63.

FRANCE
DISTRIBUTOR: Elle Tricot: 8 rue du Coq, 67000 Strasbourg.
Tel: 03 88 23 03 13.
Email: elletricote@agat.net

GERMANY
DISTRIBUTOR: Wolle & Design, Wolfshovener Strasse 76, 52428 Julich-Stetternich.
Tel: 02461 54735.

HOLLAND
DISTRIBUTOR: de Afstap, Oude Leliestraat 12, 1015 AW Amsterdam.
Tel: 020-623 1445.

HONG KONG
DISTRIBUTOR: East Unity Co Ltd, Room 902, Block A, Kailey Industrial Centre, 12 Fung Yip Street, Chai Wan.
Tel: (852) 2869 7110.

ICELAND
DISTRIBUTOR: Storkurinn, Kjorgardi, Laugavegi 59, ICE–101 Reykjavik.
Tel: 551 8258. Fax: 562 8252.
Email: stork@mmedia.is

JAPAN
DISTRIBUTOR: Diakeito Co Ltd, 2–3–11 Senba-Higashi, Minoh City, Osaka 562.
Tel: (0727) 27 6604.

NEW ZEALAND
STOCKISTS:
Auckland: Alterknitives, PO Box 30 645, Auckland.
Tel: (64) 937 60337.
Lower Hutt: John Q Goldingham, PO Box 45083, Epuni Railway, Lower Hutt.
Tel: (64) 4 567 4085.

NORWAY
DISTRIBUTOR: Ruzicka, Hans Aanrudsvei 48, N-0956 Oslo.
Tel: (47) 22 25 26 92.

SWEDEN
DISTRIBUTOR: Wincent, Norrtulsgaten 65, 11345 Stockholm.
Tel: (08) 673 70 60.

Jaeger Yarns

UNITED KINGDOM
Jaeger Yarns, Green Lane Mill, Holmfirth,
West Yorkshire HD7 1RW, England.
Tel: (01484) 681 881.
Fax: (01484) 687 920.

USA
DISTRIBUTOR: Jaeger Yarns, 5 Northern
Boulevard, Amherst, NH 03031.
Tel: (603) 886-5041/5043.
Email: wfibers@aol.com

AUSTRALIA
DISTRIBUTOR: L & G Griffiths, PO Box 65,
Kilsyth, Victoria 3137.
Tel: 03 972 86885.

BELGIUM
Distributor as Rowan.

CANADA
Distributors as Rowan.

FRANCE
Distributors as Rowan.

GERMANY
Distributors as Rowan.

HOLLAND
Distributors as Rowan.

HONG KONG
Distributors as Rowan.

ICELAND
Distributors as Rowan.

JAPAN
DISTRIBUTOR: Puppy Co Ltd, TOC Building,
7-22-17 Nishigotanda, Shinagawa-ku,
Tokyo.
Tel: 03 3494 2395.

SWEDEN
Distributors as Rowan.

TAIWAN
DISTRIBUTOR: Green Leave Co Ltd, 6F1 No
21 Juen Kong Road, Chung Ho City,
Taipei Hsien.
Tel: (886) 2 8221 2925,

Acknowledgments

This book has been a quite a ladder to climb, particularly being my first effort. Behind the scenes of this production have been an army of busy hands and minds, this book could not have been such a pleasure to do without them.

Firstly a big thank you to Denise Bates and Lisa Pendreigh at Ebury Press. My utmost gratitude must go to Sharon Brant for her enthusiasm and loyal support in overseeing the technical side of making up the garments. Sincere thanks go to Thelma Gardner, Elaine Cockcroft, Eileen Butcher, Violet Clements, Mary Potter and Wendy Harvey for their tireless hours of knitting. To Ali, Alistair, Aziz, Istvan and Veronike for making the garments look gorgeous plus Andrew, Belinda and Yvonne Mably for their undying support and assistance plus adding to the gorgeous model list. That also includes Alan Baxter for letting us tramp around his well kept gardens and giving such warm hospitality. Added affection to Don and Anne Marie Evans for allowing us the use of their splendid property and garden for photographing the garments. Also Mr & Mrs Weare of Ellen Terry's National Trust house, Small Hythe Place, Tenderten, Kent TN30 7NG and Adrian Hall Garden Centres, Hampstead Garden Centre, Iverson Road, London NW6. Thanks to Stephen Sheard of Rowan and Jaegar Yarns, Kathleen and Kim Hargreaves and the design team at Rowan for their guidance with the *Rowan Magazine* collections. Debbie Bliss for advice, humour and good will. Kenneth & June Bridgewater of Westminster Fibres, USA for supporting and promoting my designs and workshop tours. Trisha Malcolm, Senior Editor of *Vogue Knitting Magazine* believing in me and publishing my designs.

There is a catalogue of solid friends that I would like to thank for their encouragement and pure inspiration. Anne James for her mental stimulation, Richard Wormsley for his considered advise, Candace Bahouth for her loving enthusiasm and sharing her passion for creativity. Sincere appreciation to all those who take the time to keep in touch from different corners of the world.

To Joe Toller to whom I owe gratitude for his producing such sumptuous photography and in such unreliable weather conditions. Also for a pleasure and ease to work with.

Finally love and deepest appreciation to my best friends in the world – Yvonne, Belinda and Eleanor Mably and last but not least my mentor, Kaffe Fassett.

Aren't I lucky!